To Terri,

Happy Birthday.
Don't let the calories
get to you!
Enjoy!

Love,
Cheryl Lis
1988

Marshall Field's FRANGO CHOCOLATE COOKBOOK

CB
CONTEMPORARY
BOOKS

CHICAGO · NEW YORK

Design and art direction by Georgene Sainati
Photography by Bill Hogan
Foodstyling by JeanMarie Brownson
Additional foodstyling by Jeannine M. Angio

Copyright © 1988 by Marshall Field & Company
All rights reserved
Published by Contemporary Books, Inc.
180 North Michigan Avenue, Chicago, Illinois 60601
Manufactured in the United States of America
Library of Congress Catalog Card Number: 88-23617
International Standard Book Number: 0-8092-4435-7

ACKNOWLEDGMENTS

We wish to thank the professional candy makers in our Marshall Field's Candy Kitchens. Without them the world would be without Frango Chocolates.

A Special Thanks to the following manufacturers for providing accessories for the photographed recipes:

Miller-Rogaska—Classic Ballet Stemware . . . Minton—Haddon Hall Two Tier Trivit . . . Adams Ironstone—Veruschka . . . Caleca China—Laura Rose . . . Royal Worcester China and Serveware—Evesham . . . Royal Albert China—Old Country Roses . . . Hutschenreuther China—Baronesse . . . Block China—Black Pearl and White Pearl . . . Cartier China—La Mason De Louis Cartier, Christofle Silver . . . Royal Crown Derby China—Carlton Green . . . Marshall Field's Private Collection Pie Plate and Server . . . Click Clack Plastic Products . . . Decorator House Lucite Tray . . . Villeroy and Boch China—Vieux Luxembourg . . . Marshall Field's Private Collection China Server . . . Toscany Stemware

Each of these items is available at Marshall Field & Co.

CONTENTS

1
INTRODUCTION

Frango, the quintessential chocolate, has been a Marshall Field's hallmark for nearly six decades and a Chicago landmark as famous as Wrigley Field and the Walnut Room.

Whether wrapped in a heart-shaped box for a Valentine's Day sweetheart, tucked into a child's Easter basket, or served as the elegant conclusion of a dinner party, Frango Chocolates have come to represent the epitome of fine chocolates.

Marshall Field's has been treating patrons to gourmet foods since 1890, when its first tearoom opened. In 1915, the famous Candy Kitchens were established, followed in the twenties by Marshall Field's Bakery, which was founded to cater to the store's growing family of restaurants.

A few years later, in 1929, Marshall Field's purchased the Frederick & Nelson department store in Seattle and along with it acquired the recipe for a creamy mint-centered chocolate candy then known as "Franco Mints." Marshall Field's confectioners brought the recipe home and immediately began experimenting with it. The delicious tradition was born!

Over the years, Chicagoans savored each chocolate refinement the candy kitchens concocted. In the thirties, amid headlines about General Franco and the Spanish Civil War, the Franco was renamed Frango, and by 1945, the superlative Marshall Field's Frango Mint Chocolates became one of the bestselling premium-quality chocolates in the nation: no trip to the Windy City was complete without a visit to Marshall Field's and packages of mouth-watering Frango Mint Chocolates to take home.

Frango Chocolates come in eight different special flavors and a delectable collection of shapes and sizes, from Molded Frango Chocolate Santa Clauses to layered twenty-five-pound boxes. Frango Chocolate connoisseurs can be found the world over (Carol Burnett and Neil Diamond are just two of Marshall Field's celebrity Frango Chocolate lovers). But some things haven't changed much since the first exquisite Frango candy emerged from the first chunk of dark, rich chocolate. Fine candy making remains an art, and a step into the Marshall Field's Candy Kitchens—the heart and soul of the thirteenth floor on State Street—is almost like traveling back in time to glimpse an old-fashioned confectionery. Here, Frango candy makers still insist on standards of quality that only can be achieved by hand, time-honored techniques passed down through generations of master chocolate confectioners.

First, blocks of pure chocolate are lovingly blended with premium, fresh ingredients in large kettles. This chocolate blend, which will form the smooth, dense Frango candy centers, is tempered carefully, and spread with spatulas on heavy marble slabs until it's sliced into perfect squares and left overnight to reach the exact room temperature. The next step might well be every Frango lover's ultimate fantasy: the Frango chocolate centers are drenched in a wondrous fountain of bubbling chocolate called the "enrober." As the candies emerge from the enrober, still shiny with their wet coatings of melted dark, white, or milk chocolate, candy-kitchen "stringers" await to hand mark each piece using a small wire loop. The tiny swirl the stringer fashions on the top of each glossy chocolate square indicates which Frango Chocolate flavor is encased inside. When the finished Frango candies have cooled completely, kitchen packers nestle them in paper cuffs to be tucked into the familiar Marshall Field's boxes or gift wrapped in an array of elegant samplers and festive holiday containers.

Today, the Frango Chocolates family includes eight ambrosial flavors. The classic Frango mint, available in both original milk chocolate and dark chocolate, has been joined by toffee crunch, almond, raspberry, coffee, rum, and peanut butter. Marshall Field's has even created a Frango liqueur, a perfectly silken after-dinner sweet on its own and a sumptuous ingredient in dessert toppings and for baking.

Now you can indulge your family and guests with a delicious array of Frango desserts, including some of the very same specialties served in the Walnut Room. From the delicate Frango Café au Lait to the divinely rich Frango Raspberry Chocolate Pecan Torte with Raspberry Glaze (pictured on our cover), you'll find that Frango Chocolates are a pleasure to use at home. In Marshall Field's Frango Chocolate Cookbook you'll discover dozens of quick and easy recipes, as well as a few more challenging creations, but you don't have to be an expert cook to produce superb dessert creations that are a delight to serve.

Frango desserts are perfect for entertaining. You might crown a dinner party with Poached Pears in Rum Chocoalte Sauce or luxurious dark slices of Frango Truffle Torte. And for an elegant luncheon gathering, a Frango Mint Chocolate Alexander or a chilled Café au Lait Cold Soufflé makes a memorable finale. Yet even casual meals become occasions when the sweet aroma of Frango Chocolates fills the air: when breakfast begins with freshly baked Frango Toffee Crunch Nut Coffeecake or the after-school treat is moist Frango Chocolate Brownies still warm from the oven.

We've included recipes for most flavors in the Frango family—mousses, tortes, cookies, cheesecakes, breads, soufflés, brownies, and more—along with simple tips on using these wonderful fine chocolates. You even may be inspired to try Frango Chocolates in your own favorite dessert recipes. We can't imagine a better way to send a bit of the magic of Marshall Field's Candy Kitchens back home with you.

2
INGREDIENTS AND EQUIPMENT

HOW TO USE FRANGO CHOCOLATES
STORAGE AND HANDLING

Frango chocolates are best stored at cool room temperature (70°F or below). During warm weather, the Frangos can be refrigerated or frozen. However, very sudden changes of temperature will cause a white blooming on the surface of the candy. To prevent the blooming when freezing the candy, place the sealed box in the refrigerator for at least 6 hours before and after putting it in the freezer. For extra protection from humidity, wrap the box in plastic wrap.

For your measuring convenience, there are 15 Frango Chocolates in a 5½-ounce box, or about 45 Frangos in 1 pound.

CHOPPING FRANGO CHOCOLATES

Chopping Frango chocolates properly will ensure smooth and speedy melting. As a rule of thumb, remember that the greater the surface area, the more uniform the melt. Therefore, chopped chocolate spread over the bottom of a double boiler will melt quickly and evenly, as opposed to large, unchopped pieces. If the Frango chocolates are finely chopped, they generally will be added to a warm liquid and will be incorporated more easily than coarsely chopped pieces. Frango chocolates are coarsely chopped for general melting purposes and when baked in items such as scones or cookies, to retain their shape and for greater chocolate impact.

The best instrument for chopping chocolate is a large, sharp chef's knife. Do not chop Frangos in a food processor, or they will melt from the resulting friction.

MELTING FRANGO CHOCOLATES

There are two basic methods of melting chocolate: the traditional double boiler method and the more modern microwave version. In either case, never let the chocolate heat above 125°F. Overheated chocolate "tightens" or becomes thick and grainy. If this occurs, add 1 teaspoon of solid vegetable shortening (not butter or margarine) per 2 ounces of melted chocolate and stir until smooth.

For the double boiler method, heat the chopped chocolate in the top of a double boiler over very hot, not simmering, water, stirring the chocolate occasionally until it is melted and smooth. Milk and white chocolate have high proportions of milk proteins and sugar that clump and burn easily and are melted most successfully if hot tap water (not above 125°F) touches the bottom of the top of the double boiler. Never allow water to splash into the melted chocolate. If this does happen and the chocolate tightens, try the method suggested above.

For the microwave method, place the chopped chocolate in a microwave-safe bowl and microwave at 50% energy (MEDIUM) for 2½ to 4 minutes, until the chocolate turns shiny. The chocolate will not always look melted and must be stirred well until smooth.

OTHER INGREDIENTS

FLOUR

All-purpose flour is used in all recipes, unless otherwise specified.

SUGAR

Granulated sugar is used in all recipes, unless otherwise specified. Generally, light and dark brown sugars can be substituted for each other with little difference in taste and appearance in the finished desserts. Superfine sugar (sometimes called bar sugar) is available in supermarkets and some liquor stores. You can make your own superfine sugar by grinding granulated sugar in a food processor or blender until very fine.

EGGS

USDA large eggs are used in all recipes. Always store eggs in the refrigerator. They are most easily separated when chilled; however, you will get best results in beating and cooking with room-temperature yolks and whites. Egg whites must be beaten in a very clean, grease-free bowl. Egg yolks are very delicate and will scramble quickly if added to a hot liquid. Temper the yolks by gradually beating in a small amount of the hot liquid before incorporating completely.

BUTTER

Unsalted butter, also called sweet butter, is used in all recipes. If using salted butter, decrease any salt in the recipe to taste. To quickly soften butter for creaming purposes, grate the butter coarsely into a bowl, then proceed with the recipe.

HEAVY CREAM

Unsweetened heavy cream, which generally has a slightly higher butterfat content than whipping cream, is used in all recipes. The creams are often labeled differently from state to state, but the difference between the two kinds of cream is very slight. They can be substituted for one another.

Note: Because white chocolate does not contain chocolate liquor, the Food and Drug Administration prohibits it from being labeled as "white chocolate." However, because the term is so commonly referred to and accepted throughout the cooking industry, we have chosen to identify it in this cookbook simply as white chocolate.

EQUIPMENT

DOUBLE BOILER

The double boiler is the most useful tool for the chocolate cook. You may buy a double boiler at cookware stores or improvise your own, using a heatproof bowl set over a saucepan. This method is particularly useful for large-batch recipes in which a large amount of chocolate is being melted.

FOOD PROCESSOR

The food processor is excellent for chopping nuts and grinding cookies for crusts. However, it is not recommended for chopping chocolates.

ELECTRIC MIXERS

All recipes have been tested using a hand-held electric mixer unless otherwise specified. You may use a standing heavy-duty mixer, but adjust the mixing times to compensate for the increased power. Use the visual descriptions in the recipes as guidelines to avoid over- or underbeating.

KITCHEN PARCHMENT PAPER

Silicon-coated parchment paper is becoming widely available in cookware stores and most grocery stores. Do not confuse this with artist's parchment paper. Kitchen parchment paper will ensure easy removal of sticky baked goods. Do not substitute waxed paper unless the recipes so specify.

CAKE PANS

The size of the cake pan you use is very important. The pans should be one-half to two-thirds full for best rising. All recipes in this book have been tested with 8-, 9-, or 10-inch round pans, each 1½ inches deep, unless recipes call for springform pans, which should be 2 inches deep. If possible, buy cake pans with straight sides, which make it easier to match up the frosted layers.

ORDERING FRANGO CHOCOLATES

Frango Chocolates can be ordered in one-pound boxes in any of the following flavors: mint (milk, dark, or white), toffee crunch, raspberry, almond, rum, and coffee. To order, contact Marshall Field's Personal Shopping Service at the following address:

Marshall Field's
111 North State Street
Chicago, Illinois 60602
Attn: Personal Shopping Service

Orders can be placed by phone at: (312) 899-1199

Frango Chocolates can be ordered and shipped from September 15th through May 1st. They cannot be shipped during the remainder of the year due to spoilage from high temperatures.

When placing an order, a charge will be added for shipping. Tax will be added if the Frango Chocolates are shipped to an address within the state of Illinois.

3
MOUSSES, PUDDINGS, AND TERRINES

FRANGO MINT CHOCOLATE MOUSSE WITH BRANDY

A sophisticated, elegant dessert that will get instant applause from your dinner guests.

MOUSSE
1 teaspoon unflavored gelatin
1 tablespoon plus ¼ cup cold
   water
½ cup sugar
12 Frango Mint Chocolates
   (milk) (about 4 ounces),
   chopped fine (about ¾ cup)
4 large eggs, separated, at
   room temperature
2 tablespoons brandy
1 cup heavy (whipping) cream

TOPPING
⅔ cup heavy (whipping) cream
Milk Chocolate curls
   (optional; see index)

Make the mousse:

1. In a small bowl, soften the gelatin in 1 tablespoon water. In a medium saucepan, bring ¼ cup water and the sugar to a boil over medium heat, stirring until sugar is dissolved. Increase heat to high and boil until syrupy, about 1 minute. Remove the pan from heat, add the gelatin

18

mixture, and stir until gelatin is dissolved. Add the chopped chocolates and stir until melted. One at a time, whisk in the egg yolks, beating well after each addition. Return the pan to the heat and cook the mixture over very low heat, stirring constantly, just until very hot, about 1 minute. Do not let the mixture come near the boil, or the egg yolks will scramble. Remove the pan from the heat and let the mixture stand until cool but unset. Stir in the brandy.

2. Using a hand-held electric mixer set at medium speed, beat the egg whites in a grease-free medium bowl until they start to foam. Gradually increase the speed to high and continue beating until the egg whites form soft peaks. Stir about one-fourth of the whites into the chocolate mixture to lighten it, then gently fold in the remaining whites.

3. Using a hand-held electric mixer set at medium-high speed, beat the cream in a chilled medium bowl until it forms soft peaks. Fold the cream into the chocolate and egg mixture. Divide the mousse among six wine goblets or dessert bowls. Cover with plastic wrap and chill until firm, at least 3 hours.

Make the topping:

4. Using a hand-held electric mixer set at medium-high speed, beat the cream in a chilled medium bowl until it forms soft peaks. Top each mousse with a dollop of whipped cream and garnish with the chocolate curls if desired. Serve immediately.

Advance preparation: The mousses can be made and refrigerated up to one day in advance. Add the topping just before serving.

MAKES 6 SERVINGS

FRANGO COFFEE CHOCOLATE POTS DE CRÈME

Pots de creme are always served in small cups, as these rich custards deliver a most intense mocha flavor.

1¾ cups heavy (whipping)
   cream
15 Frango Coffee Chocolates
   (about 5½ ounces), chopped
   fine (about 1 cup)
3 ounces semisweet chocolate,
   chopped fine
6 egg yolks

1. In the top of a double boiler over hot—not simmering—water, heat the cream. Add the chopped chocolates and semisweet chocolate and whisk until the chocolates are melted and the mixture is smooth.

2. Whisk the egg yolks in a medium bowl until well combined. Gradually whisk about ½ cup of the hot cream mixture into the egg yolks. Return this mixture to the double boiler and stir with a wooden spoon until thickened, about 2 minutes. Remove from heat and strain through a sieve into a medium bowl.

3. Divide the custard into eight pots de crème cups or small ramekins. Cover each with plastic wrap and refrigerate for at least 3 hours or overnight.

Advance preparation: The pots de crème can be made, covered tightly in plastic wrap, and refrigerated up to two days ahead.

MAKES 8 POTS DE CRÈME

BLACK AND WHITE PARFAITS

Old-fashioned Frango chocolate pudding lightens up with a touch of elegant white chocolate cream for an updated dessert classic.

Old-Fashioned Frango
    Chocolate Pudding, chilled
    until firm (see index)

6 ounces white chocolate,
    chopped fine
1 cup heavy (whipping) cream

White and bittersweet
    chocolate curls (optional;
    see index)
Whipped cream
Mint leaves (optional)

1. In a double boiler over very hot tap water (about 125°F), melt the white chocolate, stirring often, until smooth. (The bottom of the pan can touch the water in this case.) Remove the double boiler from the water and let the white chocolate cool to room temperature.

2. Using a hand-held electric mixer set at medium-high speed, beat the heavy cream in a chilled medium bowl until it begins to form soft peaks. Beat in the white chocolate and continue beating just until the cream is stiff.

3. Spoon alternate layers of chocolate pudding and white chocolate cream into large goblets. Spoon a dollop of the white chocolate cream on top of each parfait. Garnish with white and bittersweet chocolate curls, a dollop of whipped cream, and mint leaves if desired. Serve immediately.

Advance preparation: The pudding can be made and refrigerated up to two days in advance. Make the white chocolate cream and assemble just before serving.

MAKES 8–10 SERVINGS

OLD-FASHIONED FRANGO CHOCOLATE PUDDING

Chocolate pudding is a family favorite, and this version gets a boost from Frango Mint Chocolates.

PUDDING
2 tablespoons cornstarch
¼ cup sugar
⅛ teaspoon salt
2 cups milk
15 Frango Mint Chocolates (dark) (5½ ounces), chopped fine (about 1 cup)

2 large eggs, at room temperature
2 tablespoons unsalted butter, at room temperature
1 teaspoon vanilla extract

TOPPING
½ cup heavy (whipping) cream
2 tablespoons confectioners' sugar
½ teaspoon vanilla extract
Dark Chocolate shavings (optional; see index)

Make the pudding:

1. In a heavy-bottomed medium saucepan, combine the cornstarch, sugar, and salt. Add ⅓ cup of the milk and whisk until the cornstarch is dissolved. Add the chopped chocolates and the remaining 1⅔ cups milk and cook over medium-low heat, stirring constantly with a wooden spoon, until the mixture comes to a boil, about 4 minutes. Simmer the mixture, stirring constantly, for 2 minutes. Remove the pan from the heat.

2. In a small bowl, whisk the eggs until lightly beaten. Gradually add about 1 cup of the hot chocolate mixture to the eggs, whisking constantly until blended. Whisk the chocolate and egg mixture back into the saucepan. Return the pan to the heat and cook over very low heat, stirring constantly, until slightly thickened, about 2 minutes. Do not let the mixture come near the boil, or the eggs will scramble. Remove the pan from the heat and stir in the butter and vanilla until the butter is melted.

3. Spoon an equal amount of the pudding into goblets or dessert bowls. Place plastic wrap directly on the surfaces of the puddings to discourage skins from forming. Using a sharp knife, cut a few slits in the plastic wrap to allow the steam to escape. Allow the puddings to cool to room temperature, then chill for at least 2 hours.

Make the topping:

4. Using a hand-held electric mixer set at medium-high speed, beat the cream in a chilled medium bowl until it begins to form soft peaks. Add the confectioners' sugar and vanilla and continue to beat until it forms soft peaks.

Assembly:

5. Spoon a dollop of whipped cream on top of each pudding and garnish with chocolate shavings if desired.

Advance preparation: The pudding can be made and refrigerated up to two days in advance. Whip the cream and assemble just before serving.

MAKES 4–6 SERVINGS

FRANGO CHOCOLATE BREAD PUDDING WITH APRICOT SAUCE

A spirited brandied apricot sauce is ladled over this moist French bread pudding for a wonderful, warming dessert.

CUSTARD

2 cups half-and-half

½ cup sugar

15 Frango Toffee Crunch Chocolates (about 5½ ounces), chopped fine (about 1 cup)

3 large eggs, at room temperature

PUDDING

15 ½-inch slices day-old French bread (about 6 ounces)

APRICOT SAUCE

1½ cups dried apricots

½ cup water

⅓ cup sugar

2 tablespoons brandy (optional)

Confectioners' sugar for garnish

Make the custard:

1. In a medium saucepan, bring the half-and-half and sugar to a simmer over medium heat, stirring occasionally to dissolve the sugar. Add the chopped chocolates and whisk until the chocolates are melted and the mixture is smooth. In a medium bowl, whisk the eggs until well combined. Gradually whisk in the hot chocolate mixture and set aside.

Make the pudding:

2. Position a rack in the center of the oven and preheat to 350°F. Lightly butter the inside of an 11-inch by 7-inch baking dish. Arrange the bread slices, overlapping, in rows. Pour the reserved custard over the bread slices. Place the baking dish in a larger baking pan and place in the oven. Pour enough hot water in the larger pan to come halfway up the sides of the baking dish. Bake until the custard is set, 50 minutes to 1 hour.

Make the sauce:

3. In a medium saucepan, bring the apricots, water, and sugar to a simmer over medium-low heat. Cover and cook, stirring occasionally, until the apricots are very soft, about 15 minutes, depending on the dryness of the apricots. Transfer the mixture to a food processor fitted with the metal blade, add the brandy, and process until pureed. Return the sauce to the saucepan and keep warm over very low heat.

4. Place the confectioners' sugar in a sieve and dust the top of the pudding. Serve the pudding warm, accompanied by the warm sauce.

Advance preparation: The pudding is best served immediately. The apricot sauce can be made, covered, and refrigerated up to two days ahead. Reheat gently over low heat before serving.

MAKES 6 SERVINGS

FRANGO STEAMED PUDDING WITH BRANDIED CREAM

Your kitchen will be full of luscious aromas when you prepare this cakelike pudding, an especially appropriate dessert for cold winter nights.

PUDDING

9 Frango Mint Chocolates (milk) (about 3½ ounces), chopped fine (about ½ cup)

2 ounces unsweetened chocolate, chopped fine

6 large eggs, separated, at room temperature

¾ cup sugar

½ teaspoon vanilla extract

¼ cup flour

½ teaspoon baking powder

½ teaspoon baking soda

Pinch salt

BRANDIED CREAM

1 cup heavy (whipping) cream

2 tablespoons confectioners' sugar

2 tablespoons brandy

¼ teaspoon ground cinnamon

⅛ teaspoon ground nutmeg

1 bunch fresh mint leaves for garnish (optional)

Make the pudding:

1. Butter well the inside of an 8-cup steamed pudding mold or Bundt pan. Dust the inside with granulated sugar and tap out the excess. Butter well the inside of the mold's lid.

2. In the top of a double boiler over hot—not simmering—water, melt the chopped chocolates and unsweetened chocolate, stirring often until smooth. Remove the pan from the heat and cool until tepid.

3. In a large bowl, using a hand-held electric mixer set at medium-high speed, beat the egg yolks with the sugar until the mixture is pale yellow and forms a thick ribbon when the beaters are lifted, about 3 minutes. Beat in the melted chocolate and the vanilla. Beat in the flour, baking powder, and baking soda, just until mixed.

4. Using a hand-held electric mixer with clean, dry beaters and set at low speed, beat the egg whites in a grease-free medium bowl until they start to foam. Add the salt, gradually increase the speed to high, and continue beating until the egg whites just form stiff peaks. Stir one-fourth of the whites into the chocolate mixture to lighten it, then carefully fold in the remaining whites. Pour the batter into the prepared pan. Place the lid on the mold. (If your mold does not have a lid, or if you are using a Bundt pan, cover the top tightly with a double layer of buttered aluminum foil.)

5. Place the covered mold in a large pot. Add enough boiling water to come halfway up the sides of the mold. Cover the pan tightly and bring the water to the boil over high heat. Reduce the heat to low and steam the pudding, keeping the water at a simmer at all times and adding more boiling water as necessary, until a toothpick inserted in the center of the pudding comes out clean, about 1 hour and 45 minutes. Transfer the pudding to a wire rack and cool for 5 minutes.

Make the brandied cream:

6. Using a hand-held electric mixer set at medium-high speed, beat the heavy cream in a chilled medium bowl until it begins to form soft peaks. Beat in the confectioners' sugar, brandy, cinnamon, and nutmeg and continue beating just until the cream is stiff.

Assembly:

7. Remove the lid from the mold and invert the pudding onto a serving platter. Place the bunch of mint in the center of the pudding if desired. Slice the pudding and serve with a dollop of the brandied cream.

Advance preparation: Although best when freshly made, the pudding can be made up to eight hours in advance. Resteam the unmolded pudding in boiling water for about 20 minutes, until hot. Make the brandied cream and assemble just before serving.

MAKES 6 SERVINGS

FRANGO MINT CHOCOLATE TERRINE WITH MINT CUSTARD SAUCE

Luxurious is the only word for this state-of-the art finale,
inspired by France's Marquis au Chocolat.

TERRINE
5 tablespoons heavy
   (whipping) cream
30 Frango Mint Chocolates
   (dark) (11 ounces), chopped
   fine (about 2 cups)
1 cup (2 sticks) unsalted
   butter, at room
   temperature, cut into 16
   pieces
4 large eggs, separated, at
   room temperature
Pinch salt

MINT CUSTARD SAUCE
2 cups half-and-half
¼ cup sugar
6 large egg yolks, at room
   temperature
2 tablespoons white crème de
   menthe or ½ teaspoon clear
   mint extract

Fresh mint sprigs for garnish

Make the terrine:

1. Lightly butter the bottom and sides of an 8½″ × 4½″ × 2½″ loaf pan. Line the bottom and sides of the pan with buttered waxed paper, buttered sides facing in.

2. In a double boiler over hot—not simmering—water, heat the cream until hot. Add the chopped chocolates and stir until melted. One piece at a time, whisk in the butter, whisking well after each addition until the butter is melted and the mixture is smooth. One at a time, add the egg yolks, whisking well after each addition. Transfer the mixture to a large bowl.

3. Using a hand-held electric mixer set at medium speed, beat the egg whites with the salt in a grease-free medium bowl until they start to foam. Gradually increase the speed to high and continue beating until the egg whites form soft peaks. Stir about one-fourth of the whites into the chocolate mixture to lighten it, then gently fold in the remaining whites. Spoon into the prepared pan, cover with plastic wrap, and refrigerate for at least 8 hours or overnight.

Make the mint custard sauce:

4. In a medium saucepan, bring the half-and-half and sugar to a simmer over medium-low heat, stirring to dissolve the sugar. In a small bowl, whisk the egg yolks until lightly beaten. Gradually whisk about ½ cup of the hot half-and-half mixture into the egg yolks until blended. Pour this mixture back into the saucepan. Stirring constantly with a wooden spoon, continue cooking over medium-low heat until the custard has thickened slightly and the sauce lightly coats the spoon, about 2 minutes. Do not let the custard come near a boil, or the eggs will scramble. A candy thermometer will read about 165°F. Remove the pan from the heat and strain the sauce into a medium bowl. Cool the sauce to room temperature and stir in the crème de menthe. Cover the sauce and chill at least 1 hour.

Assembly:

5. Dip the covered terrrine briefly in hot water, about 5 seconds. Dry the outside of the terrine, uncover, and invert the terrine onto a large serving platter. Carefully peel off the waxed paper. Using a sharp, thin-bladed knife, cut the terrine into 1-inch slices and place on dessert plates. Pour some of the sauce around each slice. Place a sprig of fresh mint in the center of each slice.

Advance preparation: The terrine should be made at least one day ahead and can be made and refrigerated up to two days in advance.

MAKES 8–10 SERVINGS

On preceding page: Black and White Parfaits
At left: Raspberries 'n Cream Shortcake

4
CAKES, CHEESECAKES, AND TORTES

FRANGO MINT LIQUEUR CAKE

A cherished classic from the Marshall Field's kitchens, this liqueur cake has a moist, light crumb and makes a wonderful afternoon snack or late-night indulgence.

CAKE

1½ cups flour

1 3-ounce package vanilla pudding mix (not prepared pudding)

¾ teaspoon baking soda

¼ teaspoon salt

6 Frango Mint Chocolates (milk) (about 2 ounces), chopped fine (about ⅓ cup)

2 ounces unsweetened chocolate, chopped fine

10 tablespoons (1¼ sticks) unsalted butter, at room temperature

1 cup sugar

2 large eggs, at room temperature

1 cup cold strong brewed coffee

½ cup Frango Mint Liqueur

¾ teaspoon vanilla extract

GLAZE

¼ cup corn syrup

¾ cup Frango Mint Liqueur

Confectioners' sugar for dusting

Make the cake:

1. Position a rack in the center of the oven and preheat to 350°F. Butter well the inside of a 10- to 12-cup Bundt pan (preferably nonstick), dust the inside with flour, and tap out the excess.

2. Sift the flour, pudding mix, baking soda, and salt together into a medium bowl. In the top of a double boiler, over hot—not simmering—water, melt the chopped chocolates and unsweetened chocolate, stirring

occasionally, until smooth. Remove the double boiler from the heat and let cool until tepid.

3. Using a hand-held electric mixer set at medium speed, beat the butter until creamy. Gradually add the sugar and continue beating until light and fluffy, about 2 minutes. One at a time, add the eggs, beating well after each addition. Beat in the cold coffee, liqueur, melted chocolate, and vanilla. (The mixture may look curdled.) One-third at a time, beat in the dry ingredients until smooth. Transfer the mixture to the prepared pan and smooth the top.

4. Bake until a toothpick inserted in the center of the cake comes out clean, 45 to 60 minutes, depending on the size of your pan. Cool the cake in the pan on a wire rack for 10 minutes.

Make the glaze:

5. In a small saucepan, bring the corn syrup to a simmer over medium heat. Remove the pan from heat and stir in the liqueur.

Assembly:

6. Invert the warm cake onto a platter and unmold. Drizzle ½ cup of the glaze over the top of the cake. Let the cake cool completely, then wrap it in plastic and let stand at room temperature for 8 hours or overnight. Unwrap the cake, invert back into the Bundt pan, and drizzle the remaining ½ cup of glaze over the cake. Wrap the top of the cake in plastic and let stand at room temperature for another 8 hours. Invert the cake onto a platter. Place the confectioners' sugar in a sieve and dust over the top of the cake.

Advance preparation: The cake can be made and kept at room temperature in an airtight container up to five days ahead.

MAKES 10–12 SERVINGS

FRANGO GERMAN CHOCOLATE TOFFEE CAKE

When is the nutty, coconutty goodness of an old-fashioned
German chocolate cake even better? When it is given the added
fillip of Frango Toffee Crunch Chocolates, of course!

CAKE

6 Frango Toffee Crunch
   Chocolates (about 2
   ounces), chopped fine
   (about ⅓ cup)
2 ounces unsweetened
   chocolate, chopped fine
½ cup boiling water
2¼ cups cake flour
1 teaspoon baking soda
½ teaspoon salt

1 cup (2 sticks) unsalted
   butter, at room
   temperature
2 cups sugar
4 large eggs, at room
   temperature
1 teaspoon vanilla extract
1 cup sour milk, at room
   temperature (see note)

FROSTING

1 14-ounce can sweetened
   condensed milk
4 large egg yolks
½ cup (1 stick) unsalted butter,
   cut up
1½ cups sweetened coconut
   flakes
1¼ cups coarsely chopped
   pecans
9 Frango Toffee Crunch
   Chocolates (about 3½
   ounces), chopped fine
   (about ½ cup)
1 teaspoon vanilla extract

Pecan halves for garnish

Note: To sour milk, stir 1 tablespoon white vinegar or lemon juice into 1 cup milk and let stand at room temperature until curdled, about 30 minutes.

Make the cake:

1. Position two racks in the center and top of the oven and preheat to 350°F. Lightly butter the bottom and sides of two 10-inch round cake pans. Line the bottom of the pans with circles of waxed paper. Dust the insides of the pans with flour and tap out the excess.

2. In a small bowl, cover the chopped chocolates and unsweetened chocolate with the boiling water and let stand 1 minute. Whisk the mixture until smooth and let cool to room temperature.

3. In a medium bowl, sift together the cake flour, soda, and salt. In a large bowl using a hand-held electric mixer set at medium-high speed, beat the butter until creamy, about 1 minute. Gradually add the sugar and beat until the mixture is light and fluffy, about 2 minutes. Beat in the cool chocolate mixture until smooth. One at a time, beat in the eggs, beating well after each addition. Beat in the vanilla. One-third at a time, alternately add the dry ingredients and the sour milk, beating well after each addition and scraping the sides of the bowl as necessary. Divide the batter evenly between the prepared pans and smooth the tops.

4. Bake, switching the positions of the cakes after 20 minutes, until the cakes spring back when touched in the center and a cake tester or toothpick inserted in the center of the pans comes out clean, about 35 to 40 minutes. Transfer the cakes in the pans to wire racks and cool for 10 minutes. Invert the cakes onto the racks, carefully peel off the waxed paper, and cool completely.

Make the frosting:

5. In a heavy-bottomed, medium saucepan, combine the condensed milk and egg yolks. Add the butter and cook over medium heat, stirring constantly with a wooden spoon, until the mixture comes to a boil and

thickens, about 8 minutes. (The large amount of sugar in the milk will keep the eggs from curdling.) Add the coconut, pecans, chopped chocolates, and vanilla and stir until the chocolates are melted. Let the frosting cool until thickened slightly, about 15 minutes.

6. Place a cake layer upside down on a serving platter. Using a cake spatula, spread about 1 cup of the frosting evenly over the cake layer. Top with the second layer and frost the top and sides of the cake with the remaining frosting. Arrange the pecan halves around the edge of the top of the cake.

Advance preparation: The unfrosted cake layers can be frozen up to one month. The frosted cake can be kept at room temperature up to two days.

MAKES 10–12 SERVINGS

RASPBERRIES 'N CREAM SHORTCAKE

Shortcake and summertime go hand in hand. Cascades of fruity fudge sauce and clouds of whipped cream crown this mouthwatering creation.

SHORTCAKE
1¾ cups flour
2 tablespoons sugar
1 tablespoon baking powder
½ teaspoon salt
6 tablespoons (¾ stick) unsalted butter, cut into ½-inch pieces and chilled
¾ cup heavy (whipping) cream
1 tablespoon unsalted butter, melted

SAUCE
3 tablespoons heavy (whipping) cream
6 tablespoons (¾ stick) unsalted butter
15 Frango Raspberry Chocolates (5½ ounces), chopped fine (about 1 cup)
2 ounces unsweetened chocolate, chopped fine
2 tablespoons light corn syrup

FILLING AND TOPPING
1 cup heavy (whipping) cream
2 tablespoons confectioners' sugar
½ teaspoon vanilla extract
2 cups fresh raspberries, sweetened with sugar if desired

GARNISH
Whipped cream
Whole raspberries

Make the shortcake:

1. Position a rack in the center of the oven and preheat to 425°F.

2. In a large bowl, stir together the flour, sugar, baking powder, and salt. Using a pastry blender or two knives, cut the butter into the dry ingredients until the mixture resembles coarse meal. Stir the cream into the dry ingredients just until combined. Using your fingers, quickly knead the dough together into a ball; do not overwork the dough. On a lightly floured surface, pat the dough out into an 8-inch circle. If desired, cut with a heart-shaped cookie cutter. Transfer the circle or hearts to an ungreased baking sheet. Using a pastry brush, brush the top of the dough with the melted butter.

3. Bake the shortcake until golden brown, about 15 to 20 minutes. Transfer the shortcake on the baking sheet to a wire rack and cool for 5 minutes. Using a large spatula, transfer the shortcake onto the wire rack and cool completely.

Make the sauce:

4. In a small saucepan, heat the cream and butter over low heat until the cream comes to a simmer and the butter is melted, about 3 minutes. Remove the pan from the heat, add the chopped chocolates and unsweetened chocolate, and let the mixture stand for 1 minute. Add the corn syrup and whisk the mixture until smooth. The sauce can be served hot, warm, or at room temperature.

Make the topping:

5. Using a hand-held electric mixer set at medium-high speed, beat the cream just until it begins to form stiff peaks. Beat in the confectioners' sugar and vanilla.

Assembly:

6. Using a serrated knife, slice the shortcake in half horizontally. Using a large spatula, remove the top half and set aside. Place some of the cream over the bottom, place raspberries over the cream, and replace the top. Cut the shortcake into wedges and serve each portion with the sauce and a dollop of the whipped cream. Garnish with whole raspberries.

Advance preparation: The shortcake can be prepared up to eight hours ahead, wrapped in plastic, and refrigerated. The sauce can be made up to two days ahead and reheated, stirring over very low heat. Whip the cream and assemble just before serving.

MAKES 6–8 SERVINGS

SPICY CARROT CAKE WITH FRANGO ALMOND FROSTING

A healthful cake full of spices and Frango buttercream frosting.
Easy to make, even easier to eat—the ultimate snackin' cake.

CARROT CAKE

1¾ cups flour
¾ cup whole-wheat flour
2 teaspoons baking soda
1 teaspoon salt
½ teaspoon ground cinnamon
½ teaspoon ground nutmeg
¼ teaspoon ground cloves
1 cup light brown sugar
1 cup sugar
1 cup vegetable oil
2 teaspoons vanilla extract

2 large eggs
2 cups grated carrots (about 1
    pound carrots, peeled,
    trimmed, and grated)
1 8¾-ounce can crushed
    sweetened pineapple, well
    drained
½ cup dark raisins
½ cup blanched slivered
    almonds, toasted (see index)

FRANGO ALMOND FROSTING

9 Frango Almond Chocolates
    (about 3½ ounces), chopped
    fine (about ½ cup)
3 cups confectioners' sugar,
    sifted
4 tablespoons (½ stick)
    unsalted butter, at room
    temperature
¼ teaspoon almond extract
½ cup sliced almonds for
    garnish

Make the carrot cake:

1. Position a rack in the center of the oven and preheat to 350°F. Butter and flour the inside of a 9-inch by 13-inch baking pan.

2. Sift the flours, baking soda, salt, cinnamon, nutmeg, and cloves into a medium bowl. Using a hand-held electric mixer set at medium speed, beat the sugars, vegetable oil, vanilla, and eggs until well mixed, about 1 minute. Using a wooden spoon, stir in the flour mixture. Stir in the carrots, pineapple, raisins, and almonds. Spread the batter evenly in the prepared pan.

3. Bake until the cake springs back when touched lightly in the center, about 55 to 60 minutes. Cool the cake completely in the pan on a wire rack.

Make the Frango almond frosting:

4. In the top part of a double boiler, over hot—not simmering—water, melt the chocolates, stirring often until smooth. Remove the double boiler from the heat and let the chocolate cool to room temperature.

5. Using a hand-held electric mixer set at medium speed, beat the confectioners' sugar, butter, almond extract, and cooled chocolate until smooth. Using a cake spatula, spread the frosting evenly over the top of the cooled cake. Sprinkle the top of the frosting with the sliced almonds. Refrigerate the cake until the frosting is set, about 30 minutes. Cut the cake into 16 2¼- by 3¼-inch rectangles.

Advance preparation: The cake can be made, covered tightly, and kept at room temperature up to two days ahead.

MAKES 16 SERVINGS

TRIPLE-TREAT CHOCOLATE LAYER CAKE

Three light, moist layers of Frango-flavored dark chocolate
covered with a minty frosting make this an irresistible addition to
any cake lover's "greatest hits" list.

CAKE

6 Frango Mint Chocolates (dark) (about 2 ounces), chopped fine (about ⅓ cup)

2 ounces unsweetened chocolate, chopped fine

½ cup boiling water

2½ cups sifted cake flour

¼ cup unsweetened, nonalkalized (not Dutch-process) cocoa powder

1 teaspoon baking soda

½ teaspoon salt

1 cup (2 sticks) unsalted butter, at room temperature

2 cups sugar

4 large eggs, at room temperature

¾ teaspoon vanilla extract

1 cup buttermilk, at room temperature

FROSTING

12 Frango Mint Chocolates (dark) (about 4 ounces), chopped fine (about ¾ cup)

2 ounces unsweetened chocolate, chopped fine

2 cups plus 4 tablespoons (4½ sticks) unsalted butter, at cool room temperature

1 cup plus 2 tablespoons confectioners' sugar, sifted

15 Frango Mint Chocolates (dark) (5½ ounces), chopped fine (about 1 cup) for garnish (optional)

Make the cake:

1. Position two racks in the center and top of the oven and preheat to 350°F. Lightly butter the bottom and sides of three 9-inch round cake pans. Line the bottom of the pans with circles of waxed paper. Dust the insides of the pans with flour and tap out the excess.

2. In a small bowl, cover the chopped chocolates and unsweetened chocolate with the boiling water and let stand 1 minute. Whisk the mixture until smooth and let cool to room temperature.

3. In a medium bowl, sift together the cake flour, cocoa, soda, and salt. Using a hand-held electric mixer set at medium-high speed, beat the butter until creamy, about 1 minute. Gradually add the sugar and beat until the mixture is light and fluffy, about 2 minutes. One at a time, add the eggs, beating well after each addition. Beat in the vanilla. One-third at a time, alternately add the flour mixture and the buttermilk, beating well after each addition and scraping the sides of the bowl with a rubber spatula as necessary. Divide the batter evenly among the three prepared pans and smooth the tops.

4. Bake, switching the positions of the cakes from front to back and top to bottom after 15 minutes, until the cakes spring back when lightly touched in the center and a cake tester or toothpick inserted in the center of the pans comes out clean, about 30 to 35 minutes. Transfer the cakes in the pans to wire racks and cool for 10 minutes. Invert the cakes onto the racks, carefully peel off the waxed paper circles, and cool completely.

Make the frosting:

5. In a double boiler over hot—not simmering—water, melt the chopped chocolates and the unsweetened chocolate, stirring often until smooth. Remove the pan from the heat and let stand until cool but still liquid.

6. Using a hand-held electric mixer set at medium-high speed, beat the butter until creamy, about 1 minute. Reduce the speed to low and gradually add the confectioners' sugar. Increase the speed to medium-high and beat the mixture until light and fluffy, about 2 minutes. Add the cooled chocolate mixture and beat, scraping the sides of the bowl with a rubber spatula, until smooth.

7. Place one cake layer upside down on a serving platter. Using a cake spatula, spread about 1 cup of the frosting evenly over the cake layer. Top with a second layer and spread with another cup of frosting. Top with the third cake layer, placed upside down. Evenly frost the top and sides of the cake with the remaining frosting. Sprinkle the top of the cake with additional chopped Frango chocolates if desired. Or, pipe buttercream frosting around the edge of cake. Garnish with a buttercream rose if desired.

Advance preparation: The unfrosted cake layers can be frozen, wrapped tightly, up to one month. The frosted cake can be kept, covered, at room temperature for up to two days.

MAKES 10–12 SERVINGS

At right: Triple-Treat Chocolate Layer Cake
On following page: Toffee Marble Cheesecake

CHOCOLATE ALMOND DACQUOISE

Two wafers of crisp almond meringue with an easy
chocolate-almond buttercream filling.

DACQUOISE
¼ cup blanched slivered
  almonds
¾ cup superfine sugar
3 large egg whites, at room
  temperature
Pinch cream of tartar
Pinch salt
⅓ cup sifted cornstarch

BUTTERCREAM
30 Frango Almond
  Chocolates (about 11
  ounces), chopped fine
  (about 2 cups)
2 ounces unsweetened
  chocolate, chopped fine
1 cup (2 sticks) unsalted
  butter, at cool room
  temperature

2 egg yolks
1 teaspoon vanilla extract

Unsweetened cocoa powder
  for dusting

Make the dacquoise:

1. Position two racks in the center and top third of the oven and
preheat to 325°F. Line two baking sheets with kitchen parchment paper.
(You may also use waxed paper, lightly buttered and floured.) Using an 8-
inch round cake pan as a guide, draw one circle on each baking sheet.

2. Combine the almonds and ¼ cup of the sugar in a food processor fitted with the metal blade and pulse until the almonds are very finely chopped. Set aside.

3. Using a hand-held electric mixer set at low speed, beat the egg whites in a grease-free medium bowl until they start to foam. Add the cream of tartar and salt, gradually increase the speed to high, and continue beating until the egg whites form soft peaks. One tablespoon at a time, add the remaining ½ cup superfine sugar, continuing to beat until the whites are very stiff. Using a rubber spatula, fold in the almond-sugar mixture and cornstarch until well combined.

4. Transfer the meringue to a pastry bag fitted with a star tip with a ½-inch opening, such as Ateco Number 5. Holding the bag about 2 inches from the baking sheet, pipe the meringue into two spirals inside each of the marked circles on the baking sheets. Using a cake spatula, spread the meringue evenly within each circle.

5. Bake the meringues until crisp and golden brown, about 25 minutes. Transfer the dacquoise layers on the parchment paper to wire racks to cool completely. Peel the parchment paper from the layers and discard.

Make the buttercream:

6. In the top of a double boiler over hot—not simmering—water, melt the chocolates and unsweetened chocolate, stirring occasionally, until smooth. Remove the pan from the heat and let cool completely.

7. Using a hand-held electric mixer set at medium speed, beat the butter until creamy. Beat in the cooled chocolates. One at a time, beat in the egg yolks, mixing well until smooth. Beat in the vanilla.

Assembly:

8. Place one dacquoise layer on a serving platter. Transfer the buttercream to a pastry bag fitted with a star tip with a ½-inch opening, such as Ateco Number 5. Pipe the buttercream in rosettes around the edge of the dacquoise layer. Pipe the remaining buttercream inside of the buttercream border. Refrigerate the dacquoise layer until the buttercream is firmer, about 10 minutes. Place the second dacquoise layer on top of the buttercream and press lightly to adhere. Cover the dacquoise with plastic wrap and refrigerate until the buttercream is firm, about 30 minutes. Place a decorative paper doily on top of the dacquoise. Place the cocoa powder in a sieve and sift over the top of the doily. Carefully lift the doily, leaving the cocoa design intact. To serve, use a serrated knife to cut the dacquoise into wedges.

Advance preparation: The dacquoise can be assembled, covered with plastic wrap, and refrigerated up to two days ahead. The meringue layers may soften and become chewy.

MAKES 6–8 SERVINGS

FRANGO BERRY TRIFLE

The trifle is England's entry in the Dessert Hall of Fame—an
elaborate medley of pound cake, rum, berries, jam, chocolate
custard sauce, and whipped cream.

CHOCOLATE CUSTARD SAUCE
2 cups half-and-half
2 tablespoons sugar
6 large egg yolks, at room
temperature
6 Frango Rum Chocolates
(about 2 ounces), chopped
fine (about ⅓ cup)

TRIFLE
1 store-bought pound cake,
about 11 ounces, cut
crosswise into 14 slices
2 tablespoons strawberry jam
6 tablespoons dark rum
1 pint strawberries, rinsed,
stemmed, and sliced

TOPPING
1 cup heavy (whipping) cream
2 tablespoons confectioners'
sugar
½ teaspoon vanilla extract
Whole strawberries for
garnish
Fresh mint leaves for garnish
(optional)

Make the chocolate custard sauce:

1. In a heavy-bottomed, medium saucepan, bring the half-and-half
and sugar to a simmer over medium-low heat, stirring often to dissolve the
sugar. In a small bowl, whisk the egg yolks until lightly beaten. Gradually
whisk about one-fourth of the hot cream mixture into the egg yolks. Pour
the cream and egg mixture back into the saucepan and cook over low heat,

stirring constantly with a wooden spoon, about 2 minutes. <u>Do not allow the mixture to come to a boil, or the eggs will scramble.</u> Remove the pan from the heat, add the chopped chocolates, and let stand for 1 minute. Whisk the mixture until the chocolates are melted. Strain the mixture into a medium bowl and allow to cool completely, stirring occasionally.

Make the trifle:

2. Spread one side of each pound cake slice with the jam. In a 10- to 12-cup glass bowl, arrange seven slices of cake, slightly overlapping, jam side up, in a spoke pattern in the bottom of the bowl. Sprinkle the cake slices with 3 tablespoons of the rum. Place one-half of the sliced berries over the cake slices. Pour one-half of the cooled custard sauce over the berries. Repeat the procedure with the remaining cake, rum, berries, and sauce. Cover the bowl tightly with plastic wrap and refrigerate for at least 4 hours or overnight.

Topping:

3. Using a hand-held electric mixer set at medium-high speed, beat the cream in a chilled medium bowl until it begins to form soft peaks. Add the confectioners' sugar and vanilla and continue to beat until stiff. Transfer the whipped cream to a pastry bag fitted with a large star tip with a ½-inch opening, such as Ateco Number 5. Pipe swirls of whipped cream over the top of the trifle and garnish with whole strawberries, plus mint leaves if desired.

Advance preparation: The trifle can be made, covered tightly with plastic wrap, and refrigerated, up to 1 day in advance. Whip the cream and assemble just before serving.

MAKES 8 SERVINGS

TOFFEE MARBLE CHEESECAKE

America's favorite dessert takes on a new marbled swirl form in
this rich, creamy toffee crunch cheesecake.

CRUST
1½ cups vanilla wafer crumbs
4 tablespoons (½ stick)
   unsalted butter, melted
2 tablespoons light brown
   sugar

CHEESECAKE
9 Frango Toffee Crunch
   Chocolates (about 3½
   ounces), chopped fine
   (about ½ cup)
1 ounce unsweetened
   chocolate, chopped fine
2 pounds (4 8-ounce packages)
   cream cheese

1¼ cups packed light brown
   sugar
4 large eggs, at room
   temperature
¼ cup heavy (whipping)
   cream

Make the crust:

1. Combine the vanilla wafer crumbs, butter, and brown sugar in a
food processor fitted with a metal blade and process until well blended.
Press the mixture evenly and firmly into the bottom and one-third of the
way up the sides of an ungreased 9-inch round springform pan that is 2
inches deep.

Make the cheesecake:

2. Place two racks in the center and bottom third of the oven and
preheat to 350°F. Place a baking pan on the bottom rack and fill it halfway
with hot water.

3. In a double boiler over hot—not simmering—water, melt the chocolates and unsweetened chocolate, stirring frequently. Remove the pan from the water and cool until tepid.

4. Using a hand-held electric mixer set at medium speed, beat the cream cheese in a large bowl until smooth. Add the brown sugar and blend well. One at a time, add the eggs, blending well after each addition, stopping occasionally to scrape down the sides of the bowl and the beaters. Beat in the heavy cream. Transfer 1½ cups of the cream cheese mixture to a medium bowl and set aside. Pour the remaining cream cheese mixture into the crust.

5. Whisk the cooled melted chocolates into the reserved cream cheese mixture until smooth. Spoon large dollops of the chocolate–cream cheese mixture onto the surface of the cheesecake batter. Using a knife, swirl the two mixtures together to get a marbled effect.

6. Bake until the sides of the cake rise and are beginning to brown, about 50 minutes to 1 hour. (The cake may appear underbaked but will firm upon chilling.) Transfer the cheesecake in the pan to a wire rack and cool for 10 minutes. Run a sharp knife around the inside of the pan to release the cake from the sides and cool the cheesecake for at least 2 hours. Cover with plastic wrap and refrigerate at least 4 hours. Just before serving, remove the sides of the springform pan.

Advance preparation: The cheesecake can be made and refrigerated up to two days in advance.

MAKES 10–12 SERVINGS

FRANGO
RASPBERRY CHEESECAKE

A pale pink raspberry cheesecake is encased in a chocolaty shell
atop a simple chocolate cookie crumb crust.

CHOCOLATE COOKIE CRUST

1⅓ cups crushed chocolate wafer cookies

¼ cup sugar

4 tablespoons (½ stick) unsalted butter, melted

RASPBERRY FILLING

2 cups fresh or frozen, defrosted raspberries

1 cup water

¾ cup sugar, divided

1 pound (2 8-ounce packages) cream cheese, at room temperature

2 large eggs, at room temperature

¾ cup sour cream

1 tablespoon cornstarch

1 tablespoon raspberry or black currant liqueur (optional)

GLAZE

⅔ cup heavy (whipping) cream

12 Frango Raspberry Chocolates (about 4 ounces), chopped fine (about ¾ cup)

4 ounces bittersweet chocolate, chopped fine

½ cup fresh raspberries (see note)

Chocolate leaves for garnish (see index)

Note: Although frozen raspberries may be substituted for fresh in the cheesecake filling, do not use frozen raspberries for the decoration. If fresh raspberries are not available, glaze the cheesecake without any raspberries at all.

Make the cookie crust:

1. Position a rack in the top third of the oven and preheat to 350°F. Lightly butter the bottom and sides of a 9-inch round springform pan that is 2 inches deep.

2. In a small bowl, combine the cookie crumbs, sugar, and melted butter. Press the mixture evenly on the bottom and one-third of the way up the sides of the prepared pan.

Make the raspberry filling:

3. In a heavy-bottomed medium saucepan, bring the raspberries, water, and ¼ cup of the sugar to a boil over medium heat. Reduce the heat to low and simmer, stirring often to prevent scorching, until the mixture is thick and reduced to about 1 cup, about 20 minutes. Using a wooden spoon, rub the raspberry mixture through a sieve into a bowl, discarding the seeds. Cool the raspberry mixture, stirring often, to room temperature.

4. Using a hand-held electric mixer set at medium speed, beat the cream cheese until smooth, about 1 minute. Add the remaining ½ cup sugar and beat until light and fluffy, about 2 minutes. One at a time, add the eggs, beating well after each addition. Add the sour cream, one-half of the raspberry mixture, the cornstarch and liqueur (if desired), and beat until smooth, scraping the bowl frequently. Pour one-half of the filling into the crust. Dot the surface of the filling with rounded teaspoons of the remaining raspberry mixture. Cover evenly with the remaining filling.

5. Bake for 15 minutes, reduce the oven to 325°F, and continue baking for an additional 30 minutes, until the sides of the cheesecake are puffed and beginning to brown. Run a sharp knife around the inside of the pan to release the cake from the sides. Cool the cake completely in the pan on a wire rack. Remove the sides of the springform pan. Wrap the cooled cheesecake in plastic and refrigerate for at least 4 hours or overnight.

Make the glaze:

6. In a small saucepan over medium heat, bring the cream just to the simmer. Remove the pan from the heat, add the chopped chocolates and bittersweet chocolate, and let the mixture stand for 1 minute. Whisk the mixture gently until smooth. Let the glaze cool until tepid.

Assembly:

7. Place ½ cup of the glaze in a medium bowl. Add the raspberries and fold together very gently, just to barely coat the raspberries. Place the cheesecake on the wire rack over a waxed paper–lined work surface. Spoon the glaze over the top of the cheesecake. Using a large cake spatula, spread the glaze over the top of the cheesecake, letting the excess glaze run down the sides. Smooth the glaze over the top and sides of the cheesecake. Pick up any excess glaze on the waxed paper with the spatula for glazing any bare spots if necessary. Off center, arrange the raspberries in a cluster. Arrange the chocolate leaves, radiating out from the raspberries. Refrigerate the cheesecake for 10 minutes to set the glaze.

Advance preparation: The cheesecake can be made, covered with plastic, and refrigerated up to two days ahead.

MAKES 10 SERVINGS

FRANGO MINT CHOCOLATE CHEESECAKE

Our version of a creamy chocolate cheesecake is made extra-special with milk chocolate and cool, refreshing mint.

CRUST
¾ cup graham cracker crumbs (about 7 crackers)

4 tablespoons unsalted butter, melted

1 tablespoon plus 2 teaspoons sugar

FILLING
15 Frango Mint Chocolates (milk) (5½ ounces), chopped coarse (about 1 cup)

1½ pounds (3 8-ounce packages) cream cheese, at room temperature

1 cup sugar

2 large eggs, at room temperature

⅓ cup heavy (whipping) cream

½ teaspoon vanilla extract

TOPPING
¼ teaspoon unflavored gelatin

1 tablespoon cold water

3 Frango Mint Chocolates (milk) (1 ounce), chopped fine (about 2½ tablespoons)

½ cup sour cream, at room temperature

Make the crust:

1. Combine graham cracker crumbs, butter, and sugar in a food processor fitted with a metal blade and process until well blended. Press mixture evenly and firmly into the bottom of an ungreased 8-inch round springform pan that is 2 inches deep.

Make the filling:

2. Place a rack in the center of the oven and preheat to 350°F. In a double boiler over hot—not simmering—water, melt the chopped chocolates, stirring frequently. Remove the pan from the water and cool until tepid.

3. Using a hand-held electric mixer at medium speed, beat the cream cheese in a large bowl until smooth. Add sugar and blend well. Add eggs one at a time, blending well after each addition, stopping occasionally to scrape down the sides of the bowl and the beaters. Add cooled chocolates, cream, and vanilla and beat until well mixed. Pour into the crust.

4. Bake until the sides of the cake rise and the top jiggles slightly when shaken, about 35 minutes. (The cake will appear underbaked but will firm upon chilling.) Run a sharp knife around the inside of the pan to release the cake from the sides. Cool the cake completely in the pan on a wire rack.

Make the topping:

5. In a small bowl, soften the gelatin in the cold water. Transfer the softened gelatin to a double boiler and stir over hot—not simmering—water until the gelatin is dissolved. Add the chopped chocolates and stir until melted. Remove the pan from the water and cool until tepid. Whisk the sour cream into the cooled chocolate mixture until blended. Spread the topping over the cheesecake. Cover with plastic wrap and refrigerate at least 4 hours. Remove the sides of the springform pan. Smooth the sides of the cake with a wet, hot knife.

Advance preparation: The cheesecake can be made up to 2 days in advance, covered, and refrigerated.

MAKES 8 SERVINGS

FLOURLESS FRANGO ALMOND CHOCOLATE TORTE

The irresistible combination of almonds and chocolate is
celebrated in this fabulous flourless torte, glazed with melted
Frango Almond Chocolates.

CAKE

15 Frango Almond Chocolates
   (5½ ounces), chopped fine
   (about 1 cup)
4 ounces unsweetened
   chocolate, chopped fine
6 ounces (about 1½ cups)
   blanched, slivered almonds

1 cup (2 sticks) unsalted
   butter, at room
   temperature
⅔ cup sugar, divided
6 large eggs, separated, at
   room temperature
½ teaspoon vanilla extract
¼ teaspoon salt
⅛ teaspoon cream of tartar

GLAZE

8 Frango Almond Chocolates
   (about 3 ounces), chopped
   fine (about ½ cup)
5 ounces blanched, slivered
   almonds, toasted and
   chopped coarse (about ⅔
   cup) (see index)

Make the cake:

1. Position a rack in the center of the oven and preheat to 350°F.
Lightly butter the bottom of a 9-inch round springform pan that is 2
inches deep. Line the bottom of the pan with a circle of waxed paper, then
butter the paper.

2. In a double boiler over hot—not simmering—water, melt the chopped chocolates and unsweetened chocolate, stirring occasionally until smooth. Remove the pan from the heat and cool until tepid.

3. In a food processor fitted with the metal blade, pulse the almonds 15 to 20 times, until finely ground but not oily, and set aside.

4. Using a hand-held electric mixer set at medium-high speed, beat the butter until smooth. Gradually beat in ⅓ cup of the sugar and continue beating until the mixture is light and fluffy, about 2 minutes. Beat in the egg yolks, vanilla, and salt. Beat in the cooled chocolate mixture. Beat in the ground almonds.

5. Using a hand-held electric mixer set at low speed, beat the egg whites in a grease-free medium bowl until they start to foam. Add the cream of tartar, gradually increase the speed to high, and continue beating the egg whites until they form soft peaks. Still beating, gradually add the remaining ⅓ cup of sugar and beat just until the egg whites form stiff, shiny peaks. Stir one-fourth of the beaten egg white mixture into the chocolate mixture, then gently fold in the remaining whites. Pour into the prepared pan.

6. Bake the torte just until a toothpick inserted halfway between the center and edge of the torte comes out with a moist crumb, about 40 minutes. The torte will appear underbaked. Do not overbake. Transfer the torte in the pan to a wire rack. Let cool for 10 minutes. Run a sharp knife around the inside of the pan to release the sides of the torte from the pan. Remove the sides of the springform pan. Invert the torte onto the rack and carefully peel off the waxed paper. Place another wire rack on top of the torte and invert again so the torte is right side up. Let the torte cool completely.

Make the glaze:

7. In a double boiler over hot—not simmering—water, melt the chopped chocolates, stirring frequently until smooth. Remove the pan from the heat and cool slightly.

Assembly:

8. Place the torte on the wire rack over a waxed paper–lined work surface. Spoon the glaze over the top of the torte. Using a large cake spatula, spread the glaze over the top of the torte, letting the excess glaze run down the sides. Smooth the glaze in a thin layer over the top and sides of the torte. Pick up any excess glaze on the waxed paper with the spatula for reglazing any bare spots if necessary.

9. Using a large spatula, transfer the torte to a 9-inch cardboard round or back to the springform pan bottom. Lift the torte up in one hand and with the other press the chopped nuts onto the glaze around the sides of the torte. Refrigerate the torte for 10 minutes to set the glaze.

Advance preparation: The torte can be made up to one day in advance, wrapped tightly in plastic wrap, and kept at room temperature. If refrigerated, remove the cake from the refrigerator one hour before serving.

MAKES 8 SERVINGS

At right: Frango Raspberry Chocolate Pecan Torte
On following page: Frango Napoleon

FRANGO TRUFFLE TORTE

Frango Mint Liqueur-soaked layers of chocolate genoise are piled with swirls of a whipped truffle ganache, then dusted with cocoa and garnished with chocolate shavings. Truly a work of art for your most special occasions!

CHOCOLATE GENOISE

½ cup (1 stick) unsalted butter, cut into pieces
1 teaspoon vanilla extract
½ cup cake flour
½ cup unsweetened cocoa powder
½ teaspoon salt
6 large eggs, at room temperature
1 cup sugar

CHOCOLATE TRUFFLE FROSTING

1½ cups heavy (whipping) cream
24 Frango Mint Chocolates (dark) (about 9 ounces), chopped fine (about 1⅔ cups)

½ cup Frango Mint Liqueur
Unsweetened cocoa powder for dusting
Chocolate shavings for garnish (optional; see index)

Make the cake:

1. Position two racks in the center and top of the oven and preheat to 350°F. Lightly butter the bottom and sides of two 9-inch round cake pans. Line the bottom of the pans with circles of waxed paper. Dust the insides of the pans with flour and tap out the excess.

2. In a small saucepan, melt the butter over medium heat. Pour the melted butter into a glass bowl or measuring cup. Let the butter cool for 10 minutes. Using a large soupspoon, skim off the light foam on the surface of

the melted butter and discard. Stir in the vanilla and transfer the butter-vanilla mixture to a medium bowl. In another medium bowl, sift together the cake flour, cocoa, and salt.

3. Whisk together the eggs and sugar in a large heatproof bowl. Place the bowl over a medium saucepan of simmering water. Whisking the egg mixture constantly, heat until the eggs are warm and the sugar is melted, about 3 minutes. (To test, rub a dab of the mixture between your finger and thumb.) Remove the bowl from the saucepan. Using a hand-held electric mixer set at medium-high speed, beat the egg mixture until pale yellow and almost tripled in volume and the mixture forms a thick ribbon when the beaters are lifted, about 4 minutes. Sift one-half of the dry ingredients over the whipped eggs and fold them together carefully with a rubber spatula, stopping before completely mixed. Sift the remaining dry ingredients over the mixture and continue folding, once again stopping before completely mixed. Whisk about one-fourth of the egg mixture into the butter-vanilla mixture until smooth. Pour this mixture back into the egg mixture and fold together carefully until completely mixed and no traces of dry ingredients remain. Divide the batter evenly between the prepared pans and smooth the tops.

4. Bake until the cakes spring back when touched in the center, about 25 to 30 minutes. Transfer the cakes in the pans to wire racks and cool for 10 minutes. Invert the cakes onto the racks, carefully peel off the waxed paper, and cool completely.

Make the frosting:

5. In a medium saucepan over medium heat, bring the heavy cream just to the simmer. Remove the pan from the heat, add the chopped chocolates, and let the mixture stand for 1 minute. Whisk the mixture gently until smooth, then transfer to a medium bowl. Place the bowl in a large bowl full of iced water and let the mixture stand, stirring occasionally,

until the mixture is very cold and thickened, about 15 minutes.

6. Using a hand-held electric mixer set at high speed, beat the cold chocolate mixture just until soft peaks form, about 30 seconds. Do not overbeat, or the frosting will become grainy. Proceed with the assembly immediately, or the frosting may harden.

Assembly:

7. Using a long serrated knife, trim each cake layer so the tops are level. Brush each layer with ¼ cup of the liqueur. Place one layer on a serving platter. Using a cake spatula, spread about 1 cup of the frosting evenly over the cake layer. Top with the second layer. Evenly frost the top and sides of the cake with the remaining frosting. Place the cocoa in a sieve and sift the cocoa over the top of the torte (see note). Press chocolate shavings around the sides of the torte if desired. Refrigerate the cake, covered loosely with plastic wrap, for 1 hour.

Note: For a beautiful, professional finish, use a template cocoa design to decorate your truffle cake. Using a wide-tipped felt pen, draw your design on a 9-inch round of thin cardboard (we drew a fancy F for Frango.) Make the lines of your design at least ³⁄₁₆-inch wide. Using a single-bladed Exacto knife, cut out the design, making a template. Place the template lightly over the top of the cake and sift the cocoa over the template. Carefully lift up the template, leaving the cocoa design on the top of the cake. Continue garnishing with chocolate shavings if desired.

Advance preparation: The unfrosted cake layers can be frozen up to one month. The finished torte can be kept, covered with plastic wrap and refrigerated, for up to two days.

MAKES 10–12 SERVINGS

FRANGO RASPBERRY CHOCOLATE PECAN TORTE

This sublime European-style dessert is heady with the aroma of raspberries, crunchy with buttery pecans, and bursting with dark chocolate flavor.

TORTE

- 1 cup plus 2 tablespoons (2¼ sticks) unsalted butter, cut up
- 15 Frango Raspberry Chocolates (5½ ounces), chopped fine (about 1 cup)
- 5 large eggs, at room temperature
- 1½ cups sugar
- 1 cup flour
- 4 ounces (about 1 cup) pecans, chopped fine
- 4 tablespoons framboise or raspberry-flavored liqueur
- 1 teaspoon vanilla extract
- ¼ teaspoon salt

GLAZE

- ⅔ cup heavy (whipping) cream
- 12 Frango Raspberry Chocolates (about 4 ounces), chopped fine (about ¾ cup)
- 4 ounces bittersweet chocolate, chopped fine
- 3 ounces (about ⅔ cup) pecans, chopped coarse

GARNISH

Pecan halves (optional)

Make the torte:

1. Position a rack in the center of the oven and preheat to 350°F. Butter the bottom and sides of a 9-inch round springform pan that is 2 inches deep. Line the bottom of the pan with a circle of waxed paper and butter the paper.

2. In a double boiler over hot—not simmering—water, melt the butter. Add the chopped chocolates and melt, stirring frequently until smooth. Remove the pan from the water and cool until tepid.

3. In a large mixing bowl, whisk the eggs and sugar together just until blended. Do not overmix. Whisk in the cooled chocolate mixture just until smooth. Using a wooden spoon, stir in the flour, chopped pecans, 2 tablespoons of the framboise, the vanilla, and the salt just until smooth. Do not overmix. Spoon the batter into the prepared pan and spread evenly.

4. Bake until a toothpick inserted halfway between the center and edge of the torte comes out with a moist crumb, about 1 hour. Do not overbake. The cake will appear underbaked. Transfer the torte in the pan to a wire rack. Let cool for 10 minutes. Run a sharp knife around the inside of the pan to release the sides of the torte from the pan. Remove the sides of the springform pan. Invert the torte onto the rack and carefully peel off the waxed paper. Sprinkle the torte with the remaining 2 tablespoons of framboise. Let the torte cool completely.

Make the glaze:

5. In a small saucepan over medium heat, bring the cream just to the simmer. Remove the pan from the heat, add the chopped chocolates, and let the mixture stand for 1 minute. Whisk the mixture gently until smooth. Let the glaze cool until tepid.

Assembly:

6. Place the torte on the wire rack over a waxed paper-lined work surface. Spoon the glaze over the top of the torte. Using a large cake spatula, spread the glaze over the top of the torte, letting the excess glaze run down the sides. Smooth the glaze over the top and sides of the torte. Pick up any excess glaze on the waxed paper with the spatula to use for reglazing any bare spots if necessary.

7. Using a large spatula, transfer the torte to a 9-inch cardboard round or back to the springform pan bottom. Lift the torte up in one hand and with the other press the chopped nuts onto the glaze around the sides of the cake. Press pecan halves around top, if desired. Refrigerate the torte for 10 minutes to set the glaze.

Advance preparation: The cake can be made up to one day in advance, tightly wrapped in plastic wrap, and kept at room temperature.

MAKES 10–12 SERVINGS

5
PIES, TARTS, AND PASTRIES

FRANGO BOSTON CREAM PIE

A nostalgic American dessert updated with the spirited flavor of
Frangos. Not a pie at all, but golden sponge cake, filled with a
creamy Frango-dotted custard and glazed with a Frango Rum
Chocolate icing.

SPONGE CAKE

4 large eggs, separated, at
  room temperature
¾ cup sugar, divided
¾ teaspoon vanilla extract
⅛ teaspoon cream of tartar
¾ cup sifted cake flour
¼ teaspoon salt

CUSTARD FILLING

¼ cup sugar
2 tablespoons cornstarch
3 large egg yolks, at room
  temperature
1 cup milk
½ teaspoon vanilla extract

FRANGO ICING

6 tablespoons heavy
  (whipping) cream
9 Frango Rum Chocolates
  (about 3½ ounces), chopped
  fine (about ½ cup)
½ cup sifted confectioners'
  sugar

6 Frango Rum Chocolates (about 2 ounces), chopped fine (about ⅓ cup)

Make the cake:

1. Position a rack in the center of the oven and preheat to 350°F.
Lightly butter the bottom only of a 9-inch springform pan, 2 inches deep.
Line the bottom of the pan with a circle of waxed paper. Do not grease or
flour the sides of the pan or the waxed paper circle.

2. Using a hand-held electric mixer set at medium-high speed, beat
the egg yolks with 6 tablespoons of sugar and the vanilla until the mixture
is pale yellow and forms a thick ribbon when the beaters are lifted, about 3
minutes.

3. Using a hand-held electric mixer with clean, dry beaters and set at low speed, beat the egg whites in a grease-free large bowl until they start to foam. Add the cream of tartar, gradually increase the speed to high, and continue beating until the egg whites form soft peaks. Still beating, gradually add the remaining 6 tablespoons of sugar and beat until the egg whites form stiff, shiny peaks. Stir one-fourth of the egg whites into the egg yolk mixture to lighten it. Pour the lightened egg yolk mixture on top of the remaining egg whites. Sift half of the cake flour and the salt over the egg mixture, and, using a rubber spatula, carefully fold the flour into the egg mixture, just until barely blended. (Some traces of flour will remain visible.) Sift the remaining cake flour over the mixture and carefully fold together just until thoroughly blended and no flour is visible. Transfer the batter to the prepared springform pan.

4. Bake until the cake springs back when touched in the center, about 25 to 30 minutes. Transfer the cake in the pan to a wire rack and cool for 10 minutes. Run a sharp knife around the inside of the pan to release the cake and remove the sides of the springform pan. Invert the cake onto a wire rack, carefully peel off the waxed paper, and cool completely.

Make the custard filling:

5. In a heavy-bottomed, medium saucepan, combine the sugar, cornstarch, and egg yolks. Add about one-fourth of the milk and whisk until the cornstarch is dissolved. In a medium saucepan over medium heat, bring the remaining milk to a simmer. Gradually whisk the hot milk into the egg mixture and bring to a simmer over medium heat, stirring constantly, about 3 minutes. (The cornstarch will keep the egg yolks from scrambling.) Stir in the vanilla extract. Transfer the custard to a medium bowl. Place a sheet of plastic wrap directly on the surface of the custard to

discourage a skin from forming. Using a sharp knife, cut a few slits in the plastic wrap to allow the steam to escape. Allow the pudding to cool to room temperature, then chill for at least 2 hours.

Make the icing:

6. In a small saucepan, bring the cream just to a simmer over medium heat. Remove the pan from the heat, add the chopped chocolates, and let stand for 1 minute. Whisk the mixture until smooth. Let the chocolate mixture stand until tepid. Stir in the sifted confectioners' sugar until smooth.

Assembly:

7. Using a dry pastry brush, brush the sides of the cake to remove excess crumbs. Using a long serrated knife, trim the top of the cake so it is level. Slice the cake horizontally into two equal layers.

8. Place one cake layer on a serving platter. Stir the custard filling briefly, just until smooth. (Do not whisk, or the custard will become too thin.) Using a cake spatula, spread the custard filling evenly over the cake layer. Sprinkle the filling with the chopped Frangos. Top with the second cake layer. Evenly frost the top of the cake with the icing. Refrigerate the cake until the icing is set, about 15 minutes.

Advance preparation: The cream pie can be made, covered with plastic wrap and refrigerated, up to two days in advance.

MAKES 6–8 SERVINGS

SILK PIE "A LA MENTHE"

Indulge in this smooth-as-silk, rich, chocolaty pie in a buttery pecan crust for a singular treat.

CRUST

1 cup flour
2 tablespoons sugar
2 tablespoons finely chopped pecans
⅛ teaspoon salt
5 tablespoons plus 1 teaspoon unsalted butter, chilled and cut into ½-inch pieces
1 large egg yolk, chilled
1 tablespoon ice water
¼ teaspoon vanilla extract
¼ teaspoon almond extract

FILLING

15 Frango Mint Chocolates (milk) (5½ ounces), chopped fine (about 1 cup)
2 large eggs, at room temperature
½ cup heavy (whipping) cream, chilled

TOPPING

½ cup heavy (whipping) cream, chilled
1 tablespoon white crème de menthe or 2 tablespoons confectioners' sugar
Milk chocolate shavings (see index)

Make the crust:

1. In a medium bowl, stir together the flour, sugar, pecans, and salt. Using a pastry blender or two knives, cut in the butter until the mixture resembles coarse meal.

2. In a small bowl, stir together the egg yolk, water, vanilla extract, and almond extract. Stir the liquid mixture into the dry mixture, just until the dough comes together. (If the dough seems too dry, sprinkle in additional water, 1 teaspoon at a time, until moist enough to hold together.) Form the dough into a flat disc and wrap it tightly in plastic wrap. Refrigerate the dough until well chilled, about 1 hour.

3. On a lightly floured work surface, using a floured rolling pin, roll the dough out into an 11-inch circle. Place the rolled dough over a 9-inch tart pan and ease it into the fluted edge. Fold in the edges of the dough to make a double layer and press them against the sides of the pan, making sure there are no air pockets. Trim the excess dough by pressing it against the fluted edge. With a fork, prick well the bottom of the dough. Cover the dough loosely with plastic wrap and freeze for 30 minutes.

4. Position a rack in the bottom third of the oven and preheat to 400°F. Line the crust with a piece of foil and fill it with pie weights or dried beans. Bake for 10 minutes, remove the weights and the foil, and continue to bake until uniformly golden, about 10 minutes more. Transfer the crust in the pan to a wire rack and cool completely.

Make the filling:

5. In a double boiler over hot—not simmering—water, melt the chopped chocolates, stirring occasionally, until smooth. Remove the double boiler from the heat. In a medium bowl, whisk the eggs until smooth. Whisk in the melted chocolate. Cool the chocolate mixture completely.

6. Using a hand-held electric mixer set at medium-high speed, beat the heavy cream in a chilled medium bowl just until it forms soft peaks. Stir one-fourth of the whipped cream into the chocolate mixture to lighten it, then carefully fold in the remaining cream. Pour the mixture into the cooled shell. Refrigerate the tart, loosely covered with plastic wrap, until the filling is firm, at least 4 hours or overnight.

Make the topping:

7. Using a hand-held electric mixer set at medium-high speed, beat the cream just until it begins to form stiff peaks. Beat in the crème de menthe or confectioners' sugar.

Assembly:

8. Transfer the whipped cream to a pastry bag fitted with a large star tip, such as Ateco Number 5. Pipe swirls of whipped cream around the edge of the tart. Sprinkle the whipped cream with the chocolate shavings. Serve immediately.

Advance preparation: The tart can be made one day in advance, covered with plastic wrap, and refrigerated. Assemble the tart just before serving.

MAKES 6–8 SERVINGS

CHOCOLATE COFFEE TOFFEE PIE

This is a coffee sensation gone to heaven and heaped with billows of mocha whipped cream.

CRUST

1 cup flour
¼ cup packed light brown sugar
3 tablespoons unsweetened cocoa powder
5 tablespoons butter, chilled and cut into ½-inch pieces
¾ cup chopped pecans
1 tablespoon ice water
1 tablespoon vegetable oil
1 teaspoon vanilla extract

FILLING

6 Frango Coffee Chocolates (about 2 ounces), chopped fine (about ⅓ cup)
1 teaspoon instant espresso powder
1 tablespoon boiling water
½ cup (1 stick) unsalted butter, softened
½ cup packed light brown sugar
3 large eggs, at room temperature

TOPPING

1 cup heavy (whipping) cream
2 tablespoons confectioners' sugar
1 teaspoon instant espresso powder
Chocolate curls for garnish (see index)

Make the crust:

1. Position a rack in the top of the oven and preheat to 375°F. Lightly butter the inside of a 9-inch pie plate.

2. In a medium bowl, stir together the flour, light brown sugar, and cocoa powder. Using a pastry blender or two knives, cut in the butter until

the mixture resembles coarse meal. Stir in the chopped pecans. In a small bowl, stir together the ice water, vegetable oil, and vanilla. Pour the liquid ingredients over the dry ingredients and stir together with a fork until the mixture forms a soft dough. Press the dough firmly and evenly into the bottom and sides of the prepared pie plate. Bake until the crust is set, about 15 minutes. Transfer the crust in the pan to a wire rack and cool completely.

Make the filling:

3. In the top of a double boiler over hot—not simmering—water, melt the chocolates, stirring occasionally, until smooth. Remove the pan from the heat and let cool completely.

4. In a small bowl, dissolve the coffee in the boiling water and let cool completely. Using a hand-held electric mixer set at medium speed, cream the butter and brown sugar together until light and fluffy, about 2 minutes. Beat in the cooled melted chocolate and espresso liquid. One at a time, add the eggs, beating well after each addition. Pour the filling into the cooled crust, smooth the top, and refrigerate until the filling is firm, about 2 hours.

Make the topping:

5. Using a hand-held electric mixer set at medium-high speed, beat the cream in a large chilled bowl until it starts to form soft peaks. Add the confectioners' sugar and espresso powder and beat just until it starts to form stiff peaks. Spread the topping over the filling. Garnish with chocolate curls. Serve the pie chilled.

Advance preparation: The pie can be made, covered in plastic wrap, and refrigerated up to one day ahead.

MAKES 6–8 SERVINGS

BLACK BOTTOM PIE

A simple version of this classic pie features a chocolate crumb
crust, a layer of Frango rum chocolate fudge, and a silken custard
top, gilded with chocolate curls.

CRUST
1½ cups chocolate wafer
    cookie crumbs
4 tablespoons (½ stick)
    unsalted butter, melted
2 tablespoons sugar

BLACK BOTTOM FILLING
¼ cup heavy (whipping)
    cream
9 Frango Rum chocolates
    (about 3½ ounces), chopped
    fine (about ½ cup)

RUM FILLING
5 large egg yolks, at room
    temperature
⅓ cup sugar
¼ cup flour
1½ cups milk
2 tablespoons dark rum <u>or</u> ½
    teaspoon rum extract
1 teaspoon vanilla extract

Chocolate curls for garnish
    (optional; see index)

Make the crust:

1. Position a rack in the center of the oven and preheat to 350°F.
Combine the chocolate wafer crumbs, butter, and sugar in a food processor
fitted with the metal blade and pulse until well blended. Press the mixture
firmly and evenly into the bottom and sides of a 9-inch pie plate. Bake
until the crust is just set, about 10 minutes. Transfer the crust in the pan to
a wire rack and cool completely.

At right: Cafe au Lait Cold Souffle

Make the black bottom filling:

2. In a small saucepan, bring the cream to a simmer over medium heat. Remove the pan from heat, add the chopped chocolates, and whisk until the chocolates are melted and the mixture is smooth. Pour the mixture into the bottom of the cooled crust and refrigerate until the black bottom filling is just firm, about 30 minutes.

Make the rum filling:

3. Whisk the egg yolks and sugar in a medium bowl until thickened and light, about 1 minute. Whisk in the flour. Add about ¼ cup of the milk and whisk to form a smooth paste.

4. In a heavy-bottomed, medium saucepan, bring the remaining 1¼ cups milk to a simmer over medium heat. Gradually whisk the hot milk into the egg yolk–flour mixture. Return this mixture to the pan and bring to simmer over medium heat, whisking constantly. (The flour will keep the eggs from curdling.) Reduce the heat to low and cook, whisking constantly, until the mixture is thick and very smooth, about 2 minutes. (If at any time the pastry cream becomes lumpy, remove the pan from the heat and whisk briskly until smooth again.) Remove the pan from heat and stir in the rum and vanilla. Transfer the rum filling to a medium bowl.

5. Place the bowl in a larger bowl filled with ice water and chill, stirring occasionally, until the filling is cool, about 15 minutes. Pour the rum filling over the black bottom filling in the crust and smooth the top. Place a piece of plastic wrap directly on the surface of the rum filling and refrigerate for at least 4 hours or overnight. Remove the plastic and sprinkle the top of the pie with chocolate curls if desired.

Advance preparation: The pie can be made, covered with plastic wrap, and refrigerated up to two days ahead.

MAKES 6–8 SERVINGS

At left: Frango Mint Chocolate Chunk Scones

FRANGO RUM CHOCOLATE BANANA TROPICAL TART

Fill your mind with visions of the tropics and soothe your soul
with a chocolate pastry cream mounded in a nest of toasted
coconut and topped with apricot-glazed banana slices.

COCONUT CRUST

3 tablespoons unsalted butter, softened

2 cups sweetened coconut flakes

RUM CHOCOLATE FILLING

⅓ cup sugar

3 tablespoons cornstarch

1½ cups milk

3 large egg yolks, at room temperature

9 Frango Rum Chocolates (about 3½ ounces), chopped fine (about ½ cup)

½ teaspoon vanilla extract

APRICOT GLAZE

¼ cup apricot preserves

2 tablespoons dark rum or water

3 ripe medium bananas, peeled

Make the coconut crust:

1. Position a rack in the top of the oven and preheat to 350°F. Using a paper towel, spread the softened butter over the bottom and sides of a 9-inch pie plate. Press the coconut evenly and firmly onto the bottom and sides of the buttered plate. Bake until the coconut is golden brown, about 10 minutes. Transfer the crust in the pan to a wire rack and cool completely.

Make the rum chocolate filling:

2. In a heavy-bottomed, medium saucepan, combine the sugar and cornstarch. Add one-fourth of the milk and whisk until the cornstarch is dissolved. Whisk in the remaining milk. Bring the mixture to a simmer over medium heat, whisking constantly, and cook about 3 minutes. In a small bowl, whisk the egg yolks until smooth. Gradually whisk the hot milk mixture into the yolks. Return this mixture to the saucepan, bring to a simmer over medium heat, whisking constantly, and cook about 1 minute. Remove the pan from the heat, add the chopped chocolates and vanilla, and whisk until smooth. Pour the chocolate rum filling into the cooled coconut crust. Place a sheet of plastic wrap directly on the surface of the filling to discourage a skin from forming. Using a sharp knife, cut a few slits in the plastic to allow the steam to escape. Refrigerate the pie for at least 3 hours or overnight.

Make the glaze:

3. In a small saucepan, bring the apricot preserves and rum to a simmer over low heat, stirring constantly. Cook until the last drops when poured from a spoon are sticky, about 2 minutes. Keep the glaze warm over very low heat.

Assembly:

4. Remove the plastic wrap from the tart. Cut the bananas crosswise into ¼-inch-thick slices. Arrange the banana slices, slightly overlapping, in concentric circles on top of the pie. Brush the banana slices with the warm glaze. Refrigerate the pie until the glaze is set, about 10 minutes. Serve the pie slightly chilled.

Advance preparation: The pie can be made, covered with plastic, and refrigerated up to one day ahead.

MAKES 6–8 SERVINGS

RASPBERRY DELIGHT TART

Fresh red raspberries encircle a chocolate-raspberry-filled pastry
in this surprisingly simple-to-make show-stopping tart.

CRUST

1 cup flour

2 tablespoons sugar

⅛ teaspoon salt

5 tablespoons plus 1 teaspoon
   unsalted butter, cut into ½-
   inch pieces and chilled

1 large egg yolk, chilled

2 teaspoons ice water

FILLING

½ cup (1 stick) unsalted butter

15 Frango Raspberry
   Chocolates (5½ ounces),
   chopped fine (about 1 cup)

1 large egg plus 1 large egg
   yolk

1½ cups fresh raspberries

Confectioners' sugar for
garnish

Make the crust:

1. In a medium bowl, stir together the flour, sugar, and salt. Using a
pastry blender or two knives, cut the butter into the dry ingredients until
the mixture resembles coarse meal.

2. In a small bowl, stir together the egg yolk and ice water. Stir the
liquid mixture into the dry mixture just until the dough comes together. (If
the dough seems too dry, sprinkle in additional water, 1 teaspoon at a time,
until moist enough to hold together.) Form the dough into a flat disc.

Refrigerate the dough, wrapped tightly in plastic, until well chilled, about 1 hour.

3. On a lightly floured work surface, using a floured rolling pin, roll the dough out into an 11-inch circle. Place the rolled dough over a 9-inch tart pan and ease it into the fluted edge. Fold in the edges of the dough to make a double layer and press them against the sides of the pan, making sure there are no air pockets. Trim the excess dough by pressing it against the fluted edge. With a fork, prick the bottom of the dough. Cover the dough loosely with plastic wrap and freeze for 30 minutes.

4. Position a rack in the bottom third of the oven and preheat to 400°F. Line the crust with a piece of foil and fill it with pie weights or dried beans. Bake for 10 minutes, remove the weights and foil, and continue to bake until uniformly golden, about 10 minutes more. Transfer the crust in the pan to a wire rack and cool completely.

Make the filling:

5. In a small saucepan, melt the butter over low heat. Remove the pan from the heat. Add the chopped chocolates and let the mixture stand for 1 minute. Whisk the mixture until smooth. Whisk in the egg and yolk until well combined.

6. Pour the filling into the cooled pie shell. Arrange the raspberries in an upright fashion in concentric circles in the filling. Refrigerate the tart, covered loosely with plastic wrap, until the filling is firm, at least 4 hours or overnight. Sift confectioners' sugar over the top of the tart before serving.

Advance preparation: The tart can be made one day in advance, covered with plastic wrap, and refrigerated.

MAKES 6–8 SERVINGS

FRANGO MINT TASSIES

For these bite-sized delights, chocolate mint buttercream rosettes are piped into tiny cream cheese pastry shells.

PASTRY SHELLS
3 ounces cream cheese, softened
4 tablespoons (½ stick) unsalted butter, softened
1 cup flour
2 tablespoons sugar
⅛ teaspoon salt

FILLING
⅓ cup heavy (whipping) cream
3 tablespoons unsalted butter, cut into pieces
12 Frango Mint Chocolates (milk) (about 4 ounces), chopped fine (about ¾ cup)

Confectioners' sugar for dusting

Make the pastry shells:
1. Position a rack in the center of the oven and preheat to 350°F. Lightly butter 24 1¾-inch by ¾-inch (1-ounce) mini-muffin cups.

2. Using a hand-held electric mixer set at medium-high speed, beat the cream cheese and butter together until well combined. Using a wooden spoon, stir in the flour, sugar, and salt until well combined. Gather the dough into a ball. Divide the dough into 24 balls. Place one ball in each of the prepared muffin cups. Using your fingers, firmly and evenly press the dough onto the sides and bottoms of the cups. Using a fork, pierce each pastry shell well.

3. Bake until the pastry shells are lightly browned, about 18 to 20 minutes. Transfer the shells in the pan to a wire rack and cool completely.

Make the filling:

4. In a small saucepan, bring the cream and butter just to a simmer over medium heat. Remove the pan from heat, add the chopped chocolates, and let stand for 1 minute. Whisk the mixture until smooth. Transfer the chocolate mixture to a medium bowl and place the bowl in a larger bowl filled with ice water. Chill the chocolate mixture, stirring occasionally, until thick but not set, about 15 minutes.

Assembly:

5. Place the chocolate filling in a pastry bag fitted with a star tip with a ½-inch opening, such as Ateco Number 5. Pipe rosettes of the filling into each cooled pastry shell. Refrigerate until the filling is firm, about 1 hour. Place the confectioners' sugar in a sieve and sift over the tops of the tassies. Serve the tassies slightly chilled.

Advance preparation: The tassies can be made and covered in plastic wrap up to two days ahead.

MAKES 24 TASSIES

FRANGO NAPOLEONS

Your guests will never believe that these buttery pastry creations
were not made by a French bakery! Frozen puff pastry
makes it easy.

PASTRY

1 17¼-ounce package frozen
   puff pastry (2 sheets),
   thawed

CHOCOLATE CUSTARD FILLING

⅓ cup sugar
3 tablespoons cornstarch
1½ cups half-and-half
3 large egg yolks
9 Frango Mint Chocolates
   (milk) (about 3½ ounces),
   chopped fine (about ½ cup)
½ teaspoon vanilla extract

GLAZE

1½ cups confectioners' sugar
2 tablespoons hot water
1 tablespoon light corn syrup
¼ teaspoon vanilla extract

6 Frango Mint Chocolates
   (milk) (about 2 ounces),
   chopped fine (about ⅓ cup)

Prepare the pastry:

1. Position two racks in the center and top of the oven and preheat
to 375°F.

2. On a lightly floured surface, roll out each pastry sheet to a 10-

by 15-inch rectangle. Using a dinner fork, pierce the pastry very well. Transfer the pastry to ungreased baking sheets. Bake until crisp and golden brown, about 20 minutes. Transfer the pastry to wire racks and cool completely.

Make the chocolate custard filling:

3. In a heavy-bottomed, medium saucepan, combine the sugar and cornstarch. Add the half-and-half and whisk until the cornstarch is dissolved. Bring the mixture to a simmer over medium heat, stirring constantly, about 3 minutes. In a small bowl, whisk the egg yolks until smooth. Gradually whisk the hot milk mixture into the yolks. Return this mixture to the saucepan and bring to a simmer over medium heat, stirring constantly, about 1 minute. Remove the pan from the heat, add the chopped chocolates and the vanilla, and whisk until smooth. Transfer the mixture to a medium bowl. Place a sheet of plastic wrap directly on the surface of the custard to discourage a skin from forming. Using a sharp knife, cut a few slits in the plastic to allow steam to escape. Cool the custard to room temperature, then chill for at least 2 hours.

Make the glaze:

4. In a small bowl, stir together the confectioners' sugar, hot water, corn syrup, and vanilla until smooth.

Assembly:

5. In the top part of a double boiler over hot—not simmering—water, melt the six chopped chocolates, stirring occasionally until smooth. Remove the double boiler from the heat and allow the chocolate to cool until tepid. To make an "instant" pastry bag, place the melted chocolate in a small plastic sandwich bag. Squeeze the chocolate down into one corner of the bag and twist the bag closed. Using scissors, snip a small corner of the bag open to form a 1/16-inch-wide hole to squeeze the melted chocolate through.

6. Stir the chocolate custard filling briefly, just until smooth. (Do not whisk, or the custard will become too thin.) Using a serrated knife, carefully cut each pastry lengthwise into 3 rectangles, 10 by 3¾ inches. Spread about ¼ cup of the filling on each of two pastry rectangles and top each with another pastry rectangle. Spread another ¼ cup of the filling on each of the pastry rectangles and top each pastry with another pastry rectangle. You will have two large triple-decker pastry "sandwiches," made of three layers of pastry and two of filling.

7. Using a cake spatula, spread the top of each pastry "sandwich" with the glaze. Drizzle the chocolate through the bag to form any pattern you desire. (You may even write Frango six times, spaced evenly down the length of the pastry.) You may have leftover melted chocolate. Cover the pastries loosely with plastic wrap and chill until the glaze is set and the filling is firm, about 1 hour. Using a serrated knife, cut each pastry crosswise into six rectangles, each about 1¾ by 3½ inches.

Advance preparation: The pastries can be made up to one day in advance, covered in plastic wrap, and refrigerated.

MAKES 12 NAPOLEONS

6
SOUFFLÉS AND CREPES

MINT CHOCOLATE SOUFFLÉ

A light, airy puff with refreshing, chocolaty mint goodness.

¼ cup sugar

2 tablespoons cornstarch

1 cup milk

6 Frango Mint Chocolates
(milk) (about 2 ounces),
chopped fine (about ⅓ cup)

2 ounces unsweetened
chocolate, chopped fine

¼ teaspoon mint extract

3 large egg yolks, at room
temperature

5 large egg whites, at room
temperature

Pinch salt

Unsweetened cocoa powder
for dusting

1. Position a rack in the center of the oven and preheat to 375°F.
Wrap a long sheet of aluminum foil around the outside of a 1½-quart
soufflé dish, forming a collar that rises 2 inches above the dish. Butter the
inside of the dish and the foil, dust with sugar, and tap out the excess.

2. In a heavy-bottomed, medium saucepan, combine the sugar and
cornstarch. Add about one-fourth of the milk and whisk until the
cornstarch is dissolved. Whisk in the remaining milk and bring to a simmer,
whisking constantly, over medium heat, about 2 minutes. Reduce the heat

to low and continue cooking and whisking for another minute. Remove the pan from heat, add the chopped chocolates, unsweetened chocolate, and mint extract, and whisk until the mixture is smooth and the chocolates are melted. Whisk in the egg yolks. Transfer the mixture to a large bowl.

3. Using a hand-held electric mixer set at low speed, beat the egg whites in a grease-free large bowl until they start to foam. Add the salt, gradually increase the speed to high, and continue beating until the egg whites form soft peaks. Stir one-fourth of the egg whites into the chocolate mixture to lighten it. Carefully fold in the remaining egg whites. Transfer the soufflé mixture to the prepared dish.

4. Bake until the soufflé is puffed and a long cake tester inserted into the center comes out with a moist crumb, about 45 to 50 minutes. (The longer time period will result in a firmer soufflé.) Place the cocoa powder in a sieve and sift over the top of the soufflé. Serve the soufflé immediately.

Advance preparation: The chocolate soufflé base mixture, without the egg yolks, can be prepared up to two hours ahead. Warm the mixture over low heat, stirring constantly; do not allow to become hot. Whisk in the egg yolks and proceed. Beat the egg whites and bake just before serving.

MAKES 6 SERVINGS

CAFÉ AU LAIT COLD SOUFFLÉ

A cool, not-too-sweet dessert finale, this ethereal puff of mocha
Bavarian cream rises dramatically above its serving dish to form
the perfect ending to any dinner.

COLD SOUFFLÉ
1 tablespoon unflavored
   gelatin
⅓ cup cold brewed coffee
5 large eggs, separated
½ cup sugar
1¼ cups milk
15 Frango Coffee Chocolates
   (5½ ounces), chopped fine
   (about 1 cup)
½ cup heavy (whipping)
   cream

TOPPING
1 tablespoon confectioners'
   sugar
1 tablespoon unsweetened
   cocoa powder
½ cup heavy (whipping)
   cream
Chocolate candy coffee beans
   for garnish

Make the soufflé:

1. Fold a 19-inch piece of waxed paper in half lengthwise. Tape the
folded paper tightly around the outside of a 4-cup soufflé dish about 2
inches above the rim. Lightly coat the inside of the paper with vegetable
oil.

2. In a small bowl, soften the gelatin in the cold coffee. Using a hand-held electric mixer set at medium-high speed, beat the egg yolks with the sugar until the mixture is thick and pale yellow and forms a ribbon when the beaters are lifted, about 2 minutes. In a medium saucepan, bring the milk to a simmer over low heat. Gradually whisk about ⅓ cup of the hot milk into the beaten egg yolks until blended. Pour this mixture back into the saucepan. Stirring constantly with a wooden spoon, continue cooking over low heat until the custard has thickened slightly and the sauce lightly coats the spoon, about 2 minutes. Do not let the custard come near a boil, or the eggs will scramble. A candy thermometer will read about 165°F. Remove the pan from heat. Add the chopped chocolates and gelatin and let the mixture stand for 1 minute. Whisk the custard well until smooth and the gelatin is dissolved. Transfer the custard to a medium bowl. Refrigerate the custard until cool but not set, folding often with a rubber spatula to discourage the gelatin from setting, about 45 minutes.

3. Using a hand-held electric mixer set at medium speed, beat the egg whites in a grease-free medium bowl until they start to foam. Gradually increase the speed to high and continue beating until the egg whites form soft peaks. Stir about one-fourth of the whites into the mixture to lighten it, then gently fold in the remaining whites.

4. Using a hand-held electric mixer set at medium-high speed, beat the cream in a chilled medium bowl until it forms soft peaks. Fold the cream into the chocolate and egg white mixture. Pour the soufflé into the prepared dish. Cover the top loosely with plastic wrap and chill for at least 4 hours or overnight.

Make the topping:

5. In a small bowl, sift together the confectioners' sugar and cocoa. Using a hand-held electric mixer set at medium-high speed, beat the cream in a chilled medium bowl until it forms soft peaks. Add the confectioners'

sugar and cocoa mixture and beat until stiff. Transfer the mixture to a pastry bag fitted with a large star tip, such as Ateco Number 5.

6. Carefully remove the waxed paper collar. Pipe rosettes of whipped cream around the edge of the soufflé and garnish with the candied coffee beans. Serve immediately.

Advance preparation: The cold soufflé can be made one day in advance, covered with plastic wrap, and refrigerated. Assemble the cold soufflé just before serving.

MAKES 6 SERVINGS

At right: Frango Toffee Crunch Nut Coffeecake
On following page: Pain au Chocolat a la Frango

FRANGO RASPBERRY CHOCOLATE SOUFFLÉ WITH RASPBERRY SAUCE

A light, airy soufflé dusted with powdered sugar, this chocolaty creation has a raspberry surprise in every bite and is perfect show-off company fare.

RASPBERRY SAUCE

2 cups fresh or frozen, defrosted raspberries

¼ cup superfine sugar, or to taste

3 tablespoons raspberry liqueur, such as framboise (optional)

2 teaspoons fresh lemon juice

SOUFFLÉ

¼ cup sugar

2 tablespoons cornstarch

1 cup milk

6 Frango Raspberry Chocolates (about 2 ounces), chopped fine (about ⅓ cup)

2 ounces unsweetened chocolate, chopped fine

3 large egg yolks, at room temperature

5 large egg whites, at room temperature

Pinch salt

Confectioners' sugar for dusting

Make the raspberry sauce:

1. In a blender or food processor fitted with the metal blade, puree the raspberries, superfine sugar, liqueur (if desired), and lemon juice until

smooth. Using a wooden spoon, strain and rub the sauce through a sieve, discarding the seeds.

Make the soufflé:

2. Position a rack in the center of the oven and preheat to 375°F. Wrap a long sheet of aluminum foil around the outside of a 1½-quart soufflé dish, forming a collar that rises 2 inches above the dish. Butter the inside of the soufflé dish and the foil, dust with sugar, and tap out the excess.

3. In a heavy-bottomed, medium saucepan, combine the sugar and cornstarch. Add about one-fourth of the milk and whisk until the cornstarch is dissolved. Whisk in the remaining milk and bring to a simmer over medium heat, whisking constantly, about 2 minutes. Reduce the heat to low and continue cooking and whisking for another minute. Remove the pan from the heat and add the chopped chocolates and the unsweetened chocolate. Whisk in the egg yolks. Transfer the mixture to a large bowl.

4. Using a hand-held electric mixer set at low speed, beat the egg whites in a grease-free large bowl until they start to foam. Add the salt, gradually increase the speed to high, and continue beating until the egg whites form soft peaks. Stir one-fourth of the egg whites into the chocolate mixture to lighten it. Carefully fold in the remaining egg whites.

Assembly:

5. Pour the raspberry sauce into the prepared soufflé dish. Carefully pour the soufflé mixture on top of the raspberry sauce. Place the soufflé dish in a large baking dish. Place the baking dish in the oven and pour enough hot water into the baking dish to rise 1 inch up the sides of the soufflé dish. Bake until the soufflé is puffed and a long cake tester inserted in the center comes out with a moist crumb, about 45 to 50 minutes. (The longer time period will result in a firmer soufflé.) Place the confectioners' sugar in a sieve and sift over the top of the soufflé. Serve the

soufflé immediately, spooning up some of the raspberry sauce on the bottom of the dish along with the soufflé.

Advance preparation: The raspberry sauce can be made up to two days ahead, covered, and refrigerated. The chocolate soufflé base mixture, without the egg yolks, can be prepared up to two hours ahead. Warm the mixture over low heat, stirring constantly; do not allow to become hot. Whisk in the egg yolks and proceed. Beat the egg whites and assemble just before baking.

MAKES 6 SERVINGS

FRANGO FUDGE CREPES WITH MINT SAUCE

A minty mélange of textures and tastes, thin, feathery-light crepes enfold a rich fudge filling and are served in a pool of minty custard sauce.

CREPES

1 cup flour
2 tablespoons sugar
¼ teaspoon salt
1 cup milk
3 large eggs
2 tablespoons unsalted butter, melted
Vegetable oil for cooking crepes

FUDGE FILLING

½ cup sweetened condensed milk
½ cup heavy (whipping) cream
2 tablespoons unsalted butter
6 Frango Mint Chocolates (dark) (about 2 ounces), chopped fine (about ⅓ cup)
2 ounces unsweetened chocolate, chopped fine
2 tablespoons Frango Mint Liqueur

MINT SAUCE

1½ cups half-and-half
½ cup sugar
¼ cup coarsely chopped fresh mint leaves or 2 tablespoons dried mint leaves
6 large egg yolks

GARNISH

Confectioners' sugar for dusting
Fresh mint leaves

Make the crepes:

1. In a food processor with the metal blade or a blender, place the flour, sugar, and salt and pulse two times to combine. Add the milk, eggs, and melted butter and process briefly, just until the batter is smooth. Do not overmix the batter. Transfer the batter to a small bowl, cover tightly with plastic wrap, and refrigerate until slightly thickened, about 1 hour.

2. Lightly brush the inside of a 6-inch skillet (preferably nonstick) with vegetable oil. Place the pan over medium-high heat and let the pan heat about 30 seconds, until very hot. Pour about 2 tablespoons of the batter into the pan and swirl to distribute the batter evenly, coating the bottom of the pan. Cook the crepe for about 45 seconds, until the edges are firm and lightly browned. Using a rubber spatula, turn the crepe onto a plate. Continue the procedure with the remaining batter, brushing the pan with vegetable oil before cooking each crepe and stacking the crepes on the plate, separating them with sheets of waxed paper.

Make the fudge filling:

3. In a medium saucepan over medium heat, bring the condensed milk, heavy cream, and butter to a simmer, stirring constantly. Add the chopped chocolates and unsweetened chocolate and stir until smooth. Stir in the liqueur.

Make the mint sauce:

4. In a heavy-bottomed, medium saucepan, bring the half-and-half, sugar, and mint to a simmer over medium-low heat, stirring often to dissolve the sugar. Let the cream mixture stand for 10 minutes. Strain the cream mixture through a fine sieve into a medium bowl, pressing hard on the mint leaves with a wooden spoon. (If you are using dried mint leaves, use a very fine-meshed sieve or line your sieve with a double layer of rinsed and squeezed cheesecloth.) In a small bowl, whisk the egg yolks until lightly beaten. Gradually whisk about one-fourth of the warm cream

mixture into the egg yolks. Pour the cream and egg mixture back into the saucepan and cook over low heat, stirring constantly with a wooden spoon, until the mixture has thickened slightly and lightly coats the spoon, about 2 minutes. Do not allow the mixture to come to a boil, or the eggs will scramble. Transfer the mixture to a medium bowl and allow to cool completely, stirring occasionally.

Assembly:

5. Spread about 1 tablespoon of the fudge filling over one-half of the crepe. Fold the crepe into quarters. Repeat with the remaining filling and crepes.

6. Position a rack in the center of the oven and preheat to 450°F. Arrange the crepes on a large baking sheet and cover with aluminum foil. Bake for 3 minutes, or until the crepes are heated through. Arrange three crepes on each dessert plate, ladle the mint sauce around the crepes, dust with confectioners' sugar, garnish with mint leaves, and serve immediately.

Advance preparation: The crepes can be frozen, wrapped tightly in aluminum foil, up to one month ahead. The fudge filling and mint sauce can be made, covered, and refrigerated up to two days ahead. The filled crepes can be made, covered, and refrigerated up to four hours ahead.

MAKES 6 SERVINGS

7
MUFFINS, SCONES, AND OTHER QUICK BREADS

FRANGO MUFFINS

Each oversized breakfast muffin has a melted Frango center that
doubles as a flavorful chocolaty spread.

MUFFINS

1 cup flour
¼ cup unsweetened
  nonalkalized cocoa powder,
  such as Hershey's
1 teaspoon baking powder
1 teaspoon baking soda
½ teaspoon salt
⅔ cup sugar
½ cup buttermilk, at room
  temperature

4 tablespoons (½ stick)
  unsalted butter, melted
1 large egg, at room
  temperature, lightly beaten
8 whole Frango Mint
  Chocolates (milk) (about 3
  ounces)

PECAN STREUSEL

2 tablespoons light brown
  sugar
2 tablespoons chopped pecans
1 tablespoon unsweetened
  nonalkalized cocoa powder,
  such as Hershey's
1 tablespoon flour
1 tablespoon unsalted butter,
  melted

Make the muffins:

1. Position a rack in the center of the oven and preheat to 350°F.
Line eight 2¾-inch by 1¼-inch (4-ounce) muffin tins with paper cupcake
liners.

2. In a medium bowl, sift together the flour, cocoa, baking powder, baking soda, and salt. Stir in the sugar. Make a well in the center of the flour mixture. Pour the buttermilk, melted butter, and beaten egg into the well. Using a wooden spoon, quickly stir the ingredients together, just until moistened. Do not overbeat the mixture.

3. Divide half the batter among the prepared muffin cups, using about 1 heaping tablespoon per cup. Place one Frango in the center of each cup. Do not press the Frango down into the batter. Using about 1 heaping tablespoon per muffin, divide the remaining batter among the muffin cups, spooning the batter over each Frango to cover it completely.

Make the streusel:

4. In a small bowl, stir together the brown sugar, pecans, cocoa, flour, and butter until well combined. Sprinkle the streusel evenly over the tops of the muffins, using about 1½ teaspoons per muffin. Bake the muffins for 16 to 18 minutes or until the tops of the muffins spring back when pressed lightly with a finger. Remove the muffins from the tins, cool slightly, and serve the muffins either hot or warm. To eat, cut each muffin in half and spread the warm melted Frango over the muffin.

MAKES 8 LARGE MUFFINS

FRANGO MINT
CHOCOLATE CHUNK SCONES

Perfect for breakfast or teatime; delicious warm or at room temperature for a quick on-the-go snack.

SCONES
2 cups flour
¼ cup sugar
2 teaspoons baking powder
½ teaspoon salt
6 tablespoons unsalted butter, chilled and cut into ½-inch cubes

¾ cup plus 2 tablespoons heavy (whipping) cream
1 teaspoon vanilla extract
15 Frango Mint Chocolates (milk) (5½ ounces), chopped coarse (about 1¼ cups)

GLAZE
1 large egg yolk
1 tablespoon heavy (whipping) cream

1. Position a rack in the center of the oven and preheat to 375°F. Line a baking sheet with parchment paper. Trace a 9-inch circle on the parchment.

2. In a large bowl, stir together the flour, sugar, baking powder, and salt. Using a pastry blender or two knives, cut the butter into the dry ingredients until the mixture resembles coarse meal.

3. In a liquid-measuring cup, stir together the cream and vanilla. Stir the liquid ingredients into the dry ingredients just until combined. Using your fingers, quickly knead in the chopped chocolates; do not overwork the dough. Pat the dough into the 9-inch circle on the prepared baking sheet.

Note: To make smaller, cut dough with 2½- or 3-inch round biscuit cutters. Bake as directed.

4. To make the glaze, whisk the egg yolk and cream together in a small bowl until well blended. Using a pastry brush, lightly brush the top of the dough with some of the glaze. Cut the glazed dough into eight wedges and separate the wedges slightly. Bake until the tops are lightly browned, about 20 minutes. Transfer the scones on the baking sheet to a wire rack and cool for 5 minutes. Using a spatula, remove the scones to the wire rack and cool completely or serve warm.

Advance preparation: The scones can be made up to two days in advance, wrapped loosely, and stored. Reheat if desired.

MAKES 8 SCONES

FRANGO TOFFEE CRUNCH NUT COFFEECAKE

This pleasing eye-opener, swirled with hidden pockets of chocolate and nuts, will be welcome at any time of day.

FILLING
12 Frango Toffee Crunch Chocolates (about 4 ounces) chopped coarse (about ¾ cup)
¾ cup chopped walnuts or pecans (about 3 ounces)
½ cup packed light brown sugar
2 tablespoons unsweetened cocoa powder

COFFEECAKE
3 cups flour
1½ teaspoons baking powder
1½ teaspoons baking soda
¾ teaspoon salt
¾ cup (1½ sticks) unsalted butter, at room temperature
1½ cups sugar
3 large eggs, at room temperature
1 teaspoon vanilla extract
2 cups sour cream, at room temperature

TOPPING
2 tablespoons confectioners' sugar
2 tablespoons unsweetened cocoa powder
¼ teaspoon ground cinnamon

Make the filling:

1. In a small bowl, combine the chopped chocolates, nuts, brown sugar, and cocoa until the chocolates are well coated with the dry ingredients. Set the mixture aside.

Make the coffeecake:

2. Position a rack in the center of the oven and preheat to 350°F.

Butter the inside of a 10-cup Bundt pan. Dust the inside of the pan with flour and tap out the excess.

3. In a medium bowl, sift together the flour, baking powder, baking soda, and salt. Using a hand-held electric mixer set at medium-high speed, beat the butter until creamy, about 1 minute. Gradually add the sugar and beat until the mixture is light and fluffy, about 2 minutes. One at a time, add the eggs, beating well after each addition. Beat in the vanilla. One-third at a time, alternately add the dry ingredients and the sour cream, beating well after each addition and scraping down the sides of the bowl with a rubber spatula as necessary.

4. Spoon one-third of the batter into the prepared pan. Sprinkle one-half of the reserved Frango-nut filling over the batter. Spoon another third of the batter over the Frango-nut filling. Sprinkle the remaining Frango-nut filling over the batter.

5. Spoon the remaining batter over the Frango-nut filling, covering the dry mixture completely, and smooth the top.

6. Bake the cake until a toothpick inserted into the cake comes out clean, about 1 hour. Transfer the cake in the pan to a wire rack. Let cool for 10 minutes. Invert the cake onto the rack, unmold it, and cool completely.

Make the topping:

7. In a small bowl, combine the confectioners' sugar, cocoa, and cinnamon. Sift the mixture over the top of the cake.

Advance preparation: The cake can be made up to one day in advance and stored at room temperature in an airtight container, although it is best the day it is made.

MAKES 10–12 SERVINGS

PAIN AU CHOCOLAT
A LA FRANGO

These easy-to-make breakfast rolls are perfect for drop-in guests
or a lazy morning family brunch.

1 8-ounce package refrigerated
  crescent roll dough
8 Frango Almond Chocolates
  (about 3 ounces)
1 large egg, beaten well

1. Position a rack in the center of the oven and preheat to 375°F.
2. Open and unroll the refrigerated dough. Place one chocolate in the center of each triangle of dough. Starting at the wide ends of the triangles, roll up each triangle of dough, covering the chocolates. Fold in the open flaps of dough, forming cylinders and completely enclosing the chocolates. Place the rolls, point sides down, on an ungreased baking sheet. Brush each roll lightly with beaten egg.
3. Bake the rolls until golden brown, about 18 to 20 minutes. Transfer the rolls to a wire rack to cool slightly. Serve warm.

MAKES 8 ROLLS

8
COOKIES, BROWNIES, AND CONFECTIONS

FRANGO MINT CHOCOLATE CHIP COOKIES

Freshly baked, chewy chocolate chip cookies and a glass of milk—a time-honored combination that can't be beat!

2¼ cups flour

1 teaspoon baking soda

½ teaspoon salt

½ cup (1 stick) unsalted butter, at room temperature

½ cup solid vegetable shortening, at room temperature

1 cup firmly packed light brown sugar

½ cup granulated sugar

2 large eggs, at room temperature

5 Frango Mint Chocolates (milk) (about 2 ounces), chopped very fine (about ¼ cup)

1 teaspoon vanilla extract

25 Frango Mint Chocolates (milk) (about 9 ounces), chopped coarse (about 1⅔ cups)

3 ounces pecans, chopped coarse (about ¾ cup)

At right: Frango Mint Chocolate Chip Cookies, Almond Chocolate Macaroons, and Frango Chocolate Rocky Road

1. Position two racks in the top and center of the oven and preheat to 350°F. Line two baking sheets with parchment paper or use a nonstick baking sheet.

2. Sift together the flour, baking soda, and salt. Using a hand-held electric mixer set at medium speed, cream the butter and shortening together until blended, about 1 minute. Add the sugars and cream until well mixed, about 1 minute. Beat in the eggs, very finely chopped chocolates, and vanilla. Using a wooden spoon, add the dry ingredients and stir until well blended. Stir in the coarsely chopped chocolates and pecans. Drop rounded teaspoons of the cookie dough 1-inch apart onto the prepared sheets.

3. Bake until nearly firm but still soft to the touch in the center, about 10 minutes. Using a spatula, transfer the cookies to wire racks to cool completely. Allow the baking sheets to cool before reusing with the remaining cookie dough. Store in an airtight container at room temperature.

Advance preparation: The cookies can be made up to five days in advance and stored in an airtight container.

MAKES 8 DOZEN COOKIES

At left: Frango Mint Chocolate Surprise Cookies

FRANGO SANDWICH COOKIES

These delicate, buttery gems with a melt-in-your-mouth mint
cream filling make wonderful, light teatime treats.

COOKIES
2 cups flour
1 cup unsalted butter, at room
   temperature
⅓ cup heavy (whipping)
   cream
1 cup sugar

FILLING
6 Frango Mint Chocolates
   (milk) (about 2 ounces),
   chopped fine (about ⅓ cup)
1 cup confectioners' sugar,
   sifted
2 tablespoons unsalted butter,
   at room temperature
2 teaspoons milk

Make the cookies:

1. Using a hand-held electric mixer set at medium speed, mix the
flour, butter, and cream just until blended. Gather the dough into a disc
and wrap tightly in plastic. Refrigerate the dough until firm, about 1 hour.

2. Position two racks in the center and top of the oven and preheat
to 375°F. Place the sugar in a medium bowl.

3. Working with one-third of the chilled dough at a time and keeping the remaining dough refrigerated, roll out the dough ⅛ inch thick between two sheets of lightly floured waxed paper. Using a 1½-inch round cookie cutter, cut out rounds of dough. Using a small cake spatula, transfer the rounds, a few at a time, to the bowl of sugar. Turn the rounds in the sugar to coat well. Transfer the rounds to ungreased baking sheets. Using a fork, prick each round four times. Continue the procedure with the remaining dough and sugar. (Scraps may be gathered up, chilled until firm, and rolled out to form more cookies.)

4. Bake the cookies until just set and not beginning to brown, about 8 minutes. Cool the cookies completely on the baking sheets on wire racks.

Make the filling:

5. In the top part of a double boiler, melt the chopped chocolates over hot—not simmering—water, stirring occasionally until smooth. Remove the double boiler from the heat and let the chocolate cool to room temperature.

6. Using a hand-held electric mixer set at medium speed, beat the confectioners' sugar, butter, milk, and cooled melted chocolate until smooth and spreadable.

7. Using a small cake spatula, carefully loosen the cookies from the baking sheet. Handling the cookies carefully, spread the filling between two cookies to make a sandwich. Repeat with the remaining cookies.

Advance preparation: The cookies can be baked and filled and kept at room temperature in an airtight container for up to two days.

MAKES ABOUT 4 DOZEN COOKIES

ALMOND CHOCOLATE MACAROONS

We first learned to love these melt-in-your-mouth morsels in Switzerland. A nutty Frango Chocolate filling adds a classic American flavor to these chewy favorites.

MACAROONS*
1 cup plus 2 tablespoons
  blanched sliced almonds
  (about 4½ ounces)
1 cup confectioners' sugar
1 tablespoon unsweetened
  cocoa powder
3 large egg whites, at room
  temperature

FILLING
6 tablespoons (¾ stick)
  unsalted butter
15 Frango Almond Chocolates
  (5½ ounces), chopped fine
  (about 1 cup)

Make the macaroons:

1. Position two racks in the center and top third of the oven and preheat to 350°F. Line the bottom of two baking sheets with parchment

---

*Do not try to make the macaroons on a humid or rainy day.

(not waxed) paper. (Note: Buttering and flouring the sheets is <u>not</u> sufficient for this recipe; use nonstick parchment only.)

2. In a food processor fitted with the metal blade, pulse the almonds with ¾ cup of the confectioners' sugar and the cocoa until the almonds are very finely ground.

3. Using a hand-held electric mixer set at medium speed, beat the egg whites in a grease-free medium bowl until they start to foam. Gradually increase the speed to high and continue beating until the egg whites form soft peaks. Gradually add the remaining ¼ cup confectioners' sugar and continue beating until the whites form stiff, shiny peaks. Using a rubber spatula, fold in the ground almond mixture. (The egg whites will deflate— do not be alarmed.)

4. Transfer the mixture to a pastry bag fitted with a large, plain tip, such as Ateco Number 5. Pipe out the mixture into mounds, 1 inch wide and 1 inch apart. Bake the macaroons for 8 minutes, until just set. Prop the oven door ajar and continue baking for another 8 minutes, until barely firm. (The cookies should not be baked until dry.)

5. To release the cookies from the paper, pour a small amount of water between the parchment paper and the baking sheet to moisten the parchment paper. Transfer the cookies to a wire rack and cool completely.

Make the filling:

6. In a small saucepan, melt the butter over low heat. Remove the pan from the heat and add the chopped chocolates. Let the mixture stand for 1 minute, then whisk until smooth. Transfer the chocolate filling to a small bowl and refrigerate until firm but spreadable, about 30 minutes.

7. Using a small spatula, spread about ½ teaspoon of the filling on

the flat sides of half of the cookies. Top each coated cookie with a plain cookie, pressing the flat bottoms lightly onto the filling. Store up to 1 hour at cool room temperature before serving.

Garnish (optional):

Drizzle melted Frangos over top of cookies in a decorative design, if desired.

Advance preparation: The cookies can be made up to one day ahead and refrigerated in an airtight container.

MAKES ABOUT 30 COOKIES

FRANGO LINZER COOKIES

These spicy, nutty bar cookies have become a holiday classic cookie jar favorite. The European recipe method has lots of steps, but the results are well worth the extra effort.

¾ cup toasted, skinned hazelnuts (about 3 ounces) (see index)

¾ cup sugar, divided

1½ cups flour

½ teaspoon baking powder

¼ teaspoon salt

½ teaspoon ground cinnamon

⅛ teaspoon ground cloves

½ cup (1 stick) unsalted butter, chilled and cut into 8 pieces

1 teaspoon grated lemon zest

1 teaspoon vanilla extract

1 large egg, at room temperature, lightly beaten

6 Frango Raspberry Chocolates (about 2 ounces), chopped fine (about ⅓ cup)

⅔ cup raspberry preserves, strained

1. Position a rack in the center of the oven and preheat to 350°F. Butter an 8-inch square baking pan.

2. In a food processor fitted with the metal blade, combine the toasted hazelnuts and ¼ cup of the sugar. Pulse until the hazelnuts are coarsely ground. Transfer the ground nut mixture to a medium bowl. Do not wash the work bowl.

3. Place the remaining ½ cup sugar, flour, baking powder, salt, cinnamon, and cloves in the food processor and pulse to combine. Arrange the butter evenly over the top of the dry ingredients and pulse until the mixture resembles coarse meal. Add the lemon zest, vanilla, and egg and pulse briefly, just until the dough comes together. Do not overprocess the dough. Gather up the dough into a thick disc, wrap tightly in plastic, and refrigerate until firm, about 1 hour.

4. Reserve ¾ cup of the chilled dough. Press the remaining dough evenly into the bottom of the prepared pan. Roll the reserved dough into an 8-inch square less than ⅛-inch thick (it will be very thin) between lightly floured sheets of waxed paper. Transfer the rolled dough to a baking sheet and freeze until firm, about 15 minutes.

5. In the top part of a double boiler over hot—not simmering—water, melt the chopped chocolates, stirring occasionally until smooth. Remove the double boiler from the heat and let cool until tepid.

6. Bake the dough in the prepared pan for 5 minutes, until the dough is beginning to set. Remove the pan from the oven and, using a small cake spatula, spread the melted chocolate thinly and evenly over the top of the crust. Refrigerate the crust until the chocolate is beginning to set, about 5 minutes.

7. Place the raspberry preserves in a small bowl and stir until smooth. Spread the preserves evenly over the top of the chocolate layer. Remove the rolled dough from the freezer. Using a fluted ravioli wheel or a sharp knife, cut the dough into ½-inch-wide strips. Using a small cake spatula, release the dough strips from the waxed paper and arrange the strips in a lattice pattern over the top of the preserves layer. Bake until the strips are golden brown, about 30 minutes. Cool the cookies completely in the pan on a wire rack.

8. Using a sharp knife, cut the pastry into thirds. Using a spatula, lift out each third and transfer to a work surface. Trim away any hard edges from the cookies and cut each third vertically into four bars.

Advance preparation: The cookies can be kept at room temperature in an airtight container for up to five days.

MAKES 12 COOKIES

FRANGO MINT CHOCOLATE SURPRISE COOKIES

Bite into these powdered-sugar confections to discover a hidden
Frango Mint Chocolate center!

1 cup (2 sticks) unsalted
  butter, softened
½ cup confectioners' sugar
2 cups cake flour
1 teaspoon vanilla extract
⅛ teaspoon salt
1 cup finely chopped pecans
  (about 4 ounces)
18 Frango Mint Chocolates
  (milk) (about 7 ounces),
  halved vertically
Confectioners' sugar for
  rolling

1. In a medium bowl, using a hand-held electric mixer set at medium speed, cream the butter and ½ cup confectioners' sugar together until very light in color, about 1 minute. Using a wooden spoon, stir in the cake flour, vanilla, and salt until well blended. Stir in the pecans. Loosely cover the dough with plastic wrap and refrigerate until firm enough to handle, about 1 hour.

2. Position racks in the center and top of the oven and preheat to 350°F. Completely enclose each Frango Mint Chocolate half in about 1 level tablespoon of dough. Roll the dough between your palms to form balls. Place the cookies, spaced 1 inch apart, on ungreased baking sheets.

3. Bake for 18 to 20 minutes, switching the position of the sheets after about 10 minutes, until the cookies are golden brown. Sift the confectioners' sugar into a medium bowl and roll the warm cookies in the sugar until well coated. Remove the cookies to a wire rack to cool completely.

Advance preparation: The cookies can be baked up to one week in advance and stored in an airtight container at room temperature.

MAKES ABOUT 3 DOZEN COOKIES

TOFFEE TOPPED BLONDIES

These butterscotchy blondies are even more delicious when
slathered with the Frango Toffee Crunch Chocolate topping. Try
this quick-as-a-wink topping method on your own favorite bar
cookie or brownie too!

BLONDIES
⅔ cup flour
1 teaspoon baking powder
½ teaspoon salt
4 tablespoons (½ stick)
   unsalted butter
1 cup packed light brown
   sugar
1 large egg
1 teaspoon vanilla extract
1 cup chopped pecans (about
   4 ounces)

TOPPING
15 Frango Toffee Crunch
   Chocolates (5½ ounces),
   chopped fine (about 1 cup)

Make the blondies:

1. Position a rack in the center of the oven and preheat to 350°F. Butter an 8-inch square baking pan.

2. In a medium bowl, sift together the flour, baking powder, and salt. In a medium saucepan, melt the butter over low heat. Remove the pan from the heat and stir in the brown sugar until well mixed. Beat in the egg and vanilla until smooth. Stir in the flour mixture. Stir in the pecans. Spread the batter evenly in the prepared pan.

3. Bake until a toothpick inserted halfway between the center and the edge of the blondies comes out with a moist crumb, about 25 minutes. Transfer the blondies in the pan to a wire rack and cool for 5 minutes.

Make the topping:

4. Sprinkle the top of the blondies in the pan with the chopped chocolates. Let the chocolates stand 5 minutes, until softened. Using a cake spatula, spread the top of the blondies evenly with the softened chocolates and let cool completely. Refrigerate the blondies until the topping is set, about 10 minutes. Using a sharp knife, cut the blondies into nine squares. Store in an airtight container at room temperature.

Advance preparation: The blondies can be made up to two days in advance and stored at room temperature in an airtight container.

MAKES 9 BLONDIES

FRANGO CHOCOLATE BROWNIES

Moist, fudgy, nutty—these sensational brownies will fill your kitchen with wonderful aromas.

½ cup (1 stick) unsalted butter,
   at room temperature
2 ounces unsweetened
   chocolate, chopped fine
2 large eggs, at room
   temperature
1 cup sugar
1 teaspoon vanilla extract
½ cup flour
⅛ teaspoon salt
½ cup coarsely chopped
   pecans
8 Frango Mint Chocolates
   (dark) or your favorite
   Frango flavor (about 3
   ounces), chopped fine
   (about ½ cup)

1. Position a rack in the center of the oven and preheat to 350°F. Butter an 8-inch square baking pan.

2. In a heavy-bottomed medium saucepan over low heat, melt the butter. Remove from heat, add the chopped unsweetened chocolate, and stir until the chocolate is melted. Let the mixture cool until tepid.

3. Using a hand-held electric mixer set at medium speed, beat the eggs until light and thickened, about 2 minutes. Gradually add the sugar, then beat for an additional minute. Beat in the melted chocolate mixture and vanilla. Using a rubber spatula, fold in the flour and salt. Fold in the pecans and chopped chocolates. Spread the batter evenly in the prepared pan.

4. Bake until a toothpick inserted halfway between the center and the edge of the brownies comes out with a moist crumb, about 25 minutes. Do not overbake; brownies should be moist. Transfer the brownies in the pan to a wire rack and cool completely. Using a sharp knife, cut the brownies into nine squares. Store the brownies in an airtight container at room temperature.

Advance preparation: The brownies can be made up to 2 days in advance.

MAKES 9 BROWNIES

TRIPLE-DECKER BROWNIES

This triple Frango treat starts with a fudgy brownie base that's topped with a thick, spirited frosting layer and glazed with melted Frango Mint Chocolates. Frosting lovers, beware— these are irresistible!

BROWNIE

½ cup (1 stick) unsalted butter, cut up

2 ounces unsweetened chocolate, chopped fine

2 large eggs, at room temperature

1 cup sugar

1 teaspoon vanilla extract

½ cup flour

⅛ teaspoon salt

½ cup coarsely chopped pecans

8 Frango Mint Chocolates (milk) (about 3 ounces), chopped coarse (about ½ cup)

FROSTING LAYER

3 cups confectioners' sugar, sifted

6 tablespoons unsalted butter, at room temperature

¼ cup Frango Mint Liqueur

GLAZE

9 Frango Mint Chocolates (milk) (about 3½ ounces), chopped fine (about ½ cup)

Make the brownies:

1. Position a rack in the center of the oven and preheat to 350°F. Butter an 8-inch square baking pan.

2. In a heavy-bottomed, medium saucepan over low heat, melt the butter. Remove the pan from the heat, add the chopped unsweetened chocolate, and stir until the chocolate is melted. Let the mixture cool until tepid.

3. Using a hand-held electric mixer set at medium speed, beat the eggs until light and thickened, about 2 minutes. Gradually add the sugar, then beat for an additional minute. Beat in the melted chocolate mixture and the vanilla. Using a rubber spatula, fold in the flour and salt. Fold in the pecans and chopped chocolates. Spread the batter evenly in the prepared pan.

4. Bake until a toothpick inserted halfway between the center and the edge of the brownies comes out with a moist crumb, about 25 minutes. Do not overbake; the brownies should be moist. Transfer the brownies in the pan to a wire rack and cool completely.

Make the frosting:

5. Using a hand-held electric mixer set at medium speed, combine the confectioners' sugar, butter, and liqueur until smooth. Spread the frosting evenly over the top of the cooled brownies. Cover the pan loosely with plastic wrap and refrigerate until the frosting is set, at least 2 hours.

On preceding page: Frango Chocolate Brownies
At left: Holiday Ice Cream Roulade

Make the glaze:

6. In the top part of a double boiler over hot—not simmering—water, melt the chocolates, stirring often until smooth. Remove the double boiler from the heat and allow the chocolate to cool until tepid.

7. Using a cake spatula, spread the melted chocolate thinly and evenly over the frosting layer. Refrigerate until the chocolate is firm, about 30 minutes. Using a sharp knife, cut the brownies into 24 bars, each about 2 by 1½ inches.

Advance preparation: The brownies can be made and kept tightly covered at room temperature for up to two days.

MAKES 24 TRIPLE-DECKER BROWNIES

FRANGO
CHOCOLATE ROCKY ROAD

Minty mallow nut fudge, this makes a wonderful afternoon snack
for kids of all ages.

45 Frango Mint Chocolates
(milk) (about 1 pound),
chopped fine (about 3 cups)

8 ounces large marshmallows,
cut into fourths (or
mini-marshmallows)

1 cup (about 4 ounces) pecan
halves, toasted (see index)

1. In a double boiler over hot—not simmering—water, melt the
chocolates, stirring occasionally, until smooth. Remove the double boiler
from the water and cool the chocolate until tepid.

2. Butter a baking sheet. Stir the marshmallows and nuts into the
tepid chocolate until well combined. (Stir a couple of marshmallows into
the chocolate as a test; if they melt, the chocolate is too hot and needs to
be cooled longer. If the rocky road becomes stiff and hard to stir, heat
gently over hot water until the chocolate becomes warm again.) Spoon the
mixture out onto the baking sheet. Refrigerate the rocky road until firm, at
least 4 hours. Using a sharp knife, cut the rocky road into squares.

Advance preparation: The rocky road can be made up to two weeks in
advance and stored in the refrigerator in an airtight container.

MAKES ABOUT 2 POUNDS

CRUNCHY OAT TOFFEE BARS

Chewy with coconut and oats, crunchy with chopped nuts, and
brimming with a fudgy Frango Toffee Crunch chocolate filling,
these toffee bars are impossible to resist.

CRUST

2½ cups flour

1 teaspoon baking soda

½ teaspoon salt

1 cup (2 sticks) unsalted
butter, at room
temperature

2 cups packed light brown
sugar

2 large eggs, at room
temperature

1½ teaspoons vanilla extract

2 cups uncooked oats

1 cup sweetened coconut
flakes

½ cup coarsely chopped
walnuts or pecans (about 2
ounces)

FILLING

30 Frango Toffee Crunch
Chocolates (11 ounces),
chopped fine (about 2 cups)

1 14-ounce can sweetened
condensed milk

4 ounces unsweetened
chocolate, chopped fine

2 tablespoons unsalted butter

½ teaspoon vanilla

Make the crust:

1. Position a rack in the center of the oven and preheat to 350°F.
In a large bowl, sift together the flour, baking soda, and salt. Using a hand-
held electric mixer set at medium-high speed, beat the butter until creamy,

about 1 minute. Gradually add the brown sugar and beat until light and fluffy, about 2 minutes. One at a time, beat in the eggs, then beat in the vanilla. Using a wooden spoon, stir in the flour mixture, oats, coconut, and walnuts until well mixed. Set aside.

Make the filling:

2. In a heavy-bottomed medium saucepan, combine the chopped chocolates, condensed milk, unsweetened chocolate, and butter. Cook, stirring constantly, over low heat until the chocolate is melted and the mixture is smooth. Stir in the vanilla.

Assembly:

3. Reserve 2 cups of the crust mixture. Press the remaining crust mixture evenly into the bottom of a 10½-inch by 15½-inch jelly roll pan. Using a cake spatula, spread the filling evenly over the crust. Crumble the reserved crust mixture evenly over the top of the filling.

4. Bake until the top crust is golden brown, about 25 minutes. Transfer the pastry in the pan to a wire rack and cool completely. Using a sharp knife, cut the pastry into 48 bars.

Advance preparation: The bars can be made up to three days ahead and stored in an airtight container at room temperature.

MAKES 4 DOZEN BARS

FRANGO MINT CHOCOLATE FUDGE

Sweet, creamy squares of old-fashioned goodness, fudge is the
ultimate comfort food.

4 cups sugar
1 12-ounce can evaporated
  milk
½ cup (1 stick) unsalted butter,
  at room temperature
8 ounces (about 4 cups)
  mini-marshmallows
12 ounces (about 2 cups)
  semisweet chocolate chips
21 Frango Mint Chocolates
  (milk) (8 ounces), chopped
  fine (about 1½ cups)
4 ounces German's sweet
  chocolate, chopped fine
1 teaspoon vanilla extract
60 pecan halves for garnish
  (optional)

1. Lightly butter a 15″ × 10″ × 1″ baking pan or two 9-inch square baking pans. In a heavy-bottomed large saucepan, bring the sugar, evaporated milk, and butter to a boil over medium heat, stirring constantly with a wooden spoon to dissolve the sugar. Cover the pan tightly and cook for 5 minutes. Remove the pan from the heat.

2. Add the marshmallows and let stand for 1 minute. Stir the mixture until the marshmallows are melted. Add the chocolate chips, chopped chocolates, and sweet chocolate and let stand for 1 minute. Stir the mixture until the chocolates are melted. Stir in the vanilla. Pour the fudge into the prepared pan(s) and let stand at room temperature until firm, at least 2 hours. Using a sharp knife, cut the fudge into 60 1½-inch squares. Top each square with a pecan half if desired.

Advance preparation: The fudge can be prepared up to two weeks ahead and stored in an airtight container at room temperature. The fudge keeps for two months, wrapped tightly in aluminum foil and frozen.

MAKES 60 SQUARES OF FUDGE (ABOUT 4 POUNDS)

POACHED PEARS IN RUM CHOCOLATE SAUCE

A tender, spiced pear surrounded by a pool of spirited chocolate sauce is a simple yet impressive company dessert.

PEARS
4 firm, ripe Bosc pears, peeled but not stemmed
2 cups water
1 cup sugar
Zest of 1 small lemon, removed with a vegetable peeler
1 cinnamon stick

RUM CHOCOLATE SAUCE
½ cup heavy (whipping) cream
15 Frango Rum Chocolates (5½ ounces), chopped fine (about 1 cup)
1 tablespoon dark rum

Slivered almonds for garnish

Make the pears:
1. Using a small, sharp knife, trim the bottom of each pear so it will not tip. In a medium saucepan, bring the water, sugar, lemon zest, and

cinnamon stick to a boil over medium heat. Add the pears, reduce the heat to low, and simmer, covered, until the pears are tender when pierced with the tip of a sharp knife, about 35 minutes. Let the pears cool, uncovered, in the poaching liquid. Drain the pears and refrigerate until chilled, at least 2 hours.

Make the sauce:

2. In a small saucepan over medium heat, bring the cream just to the simmer. Remove the pan from the heat. Add the chopped chocolates and let the mixture stand for 1 minute. Add the rum and whisk the mixture until smooth. The sauce can be served hot or warm.

Assembly:

3. Place a pear in the center of each of four dessert plates. Pour the warm rum chocolate sauce over each pear and sprinkle the pears with slivered almonds. Serve immediately.

Advance preparation: The pears can be made up to two days ahead, covered, and refrigerated. The sauce can be made up to two days ahead and reheated gently, stirring, over low heat.

MAKES 4 SERVINGS

9
ICE CREAMS, FROZEN DESSERTS, AND BEVERAGES

FRANGO CHOCOLATE-FLECKED
ICE CREAM

A vanilla ice cream base speckled with tiny bits of Frango
Chocolate is fantastic on its own, or try it in our Frozen
Profiteroles with Bittersweet Sauce and the Holiday Ice Cream
Roulade (see index).

2 cups half-and-half
⅔ cup sugar
4 large egg yolks, at room
    temperature
2 teaspoons vanilla extract
15 Frango Mint Chocolates
    (dark) (5½ ounces), chopped
    fine (about 1 cup)

1. In a heavy-bottomed medium saucepan, bring the half-and-half and sugar to the simmer over medium-low heat, stirring often to dissolve the sugar. In a small bowl, whisk the egg yolks until lightly beaten. Gradually whisk about one-fourth of the hot milk mixture into the egg yolks. Pour the milk and egg mixture back into the saucepan and cook over low heat, stirring constantly with a wooden spoon, until the mixture has thickened slightly and lightly coats the spoon, about 2 minutes. Do not allow the mixture to come to a boil, or the eggs will scramble. Strain the custard into a medium bowl and allow to cool completely, stirring occasionally. Stir in the vanilla. Refrigerate the custard until well chilled, at least 2 hours.

2. In a double boiler over hot—not simmering—water, melt the chopped chocolates, stirring occasionally, until smooth. Remove the double boiler from the heat and let the chocolate cool to room temperature.

3. Freeze the custard in an ice cream maker according to the manufacturer's instructions. When the ice cream is almost completely frozen, pour the cooled chocolate through the feeding space in the container—the chocolate will form shreds upon hitting the cold ice cream. Continue freezing until the ice cream is completely frozen. Transfer the ice cream to an airtight container and freeze for at least 4 hours or overnight.

Advance preparation: The ice cream can be made up to three days in advance and frozen in an airtight container.

MAKES ABOUT 1½ PINTS

HOLIDAY ICE CREAM ROULADE

In France, it's not a Winter holiday without a Bûche de Noël, an exquisite chocolate roulade cake decorated with chocolate leaves to resemble a log from the hearth. This is our do-ahead frozen rendition—perfect for entertaining.

ROULADE
15 Frango Mint Chocolates (dark) (5½ ounces), chopped fine (about 1 cup)
6 large eggs, separated, at room temperature
½ cup sugar, divided
2 tablespoons flour
3 cups Frango-Flecked Ice Cream (see index) or store-bought vanilla ice cream, slightly softened

GLAZE
⅓ cup heavy (whipping) cream
15 Frango Mint Chocolates (dark) (5½ ounces), chopped fine (about 1 cup)

GARNISH
Chocolate leaves (see index)
Store-bought chocolate twigs
Cocoa
Confectioners' sugar

Make the roulade:

1. Position a rack in the center of the oven and preheat to 350°F. Line the bottom of a 10½-inch by 15½-inch jelly roll pan with waxed or parchment paper. Butter the paper and the sides of the pan.

2. In a double boiler over hot—not simmering—water, melt the chopped chocolates, stirring occasionally, until smooth. Remove the double boiler from the water and let the chocolate cool until tepid.

3. Using a hand-held electric mixer set at medium-high speed, beat the egg yolks with 6 tablespoons of the sugar until the mixture is pale yellow and forms a thick ribbon when the beaters are lifted, about 5 minutes. Add the melted chocolate, sift in the flour, and, using a rubber spatula, fold the mixture together.

4. Using a hand-held electric mixer with clean, dry beaters and set at low speed, beat the egg whites in a grease-free medium bowl until they start to foam. Gradually increase the speed to high and continue beating until the egg whites form soft peaks. Still beating, gradually add the remaining 2 tablespoons of sugar and beat until the egg whites form stiff, shiny peaks. Stir one-fourth of the egg whites into the chocolate mixture to lighten it, then carefully fold in the remaining whites. Pour the batter into the prepared pan. Using a cake spatula, spread it in an even layer, being sure to reach the corners of the pan.

5. Bake until the center of the cake springs back when lightly pressed, about 15 minutes. Transfer the cake in the pan to a wire rack and cool for 5 minutes. Run a sharp knife around the inside of the pan to release the cake from the sides of the pan. Slide the cake out of the pan and cool on the rack for 20 minutes. Place a sheet of plastic wrap on top of the cake. Invert the cake and carefully peel off the paper. Lay the paper loosely over the cake. Using the plastic wrap as a guide, roll the cake (starting at a long end) into a cylinder and wrap tightly. Cool the roulade completely.

6. Unroll the cooled roulade and discard the paper. Using a cake spatula, spread the ice cream evenly on the roulade. Using the plastic wrap as a guide, reroll the roulade. Freeze the roulade, wrapped tightly in plastic wrap, until the ice cream is firm, at least 4 hours or overnight.

Make the glaze:

7. In a small saucepan over medium-low heat, bring the cream just to the simmer. Remove the pan from heat, add the chopped chocolates, and let the mixture stand for 1 minute. Whisk gently until smooth. Allow the glaze to cool until tepid.

8. Unwrap the roulade and place on a wire rack set over a waxed paper–lined work surface. Using a cake spatula, spread the glaze over the top of the roulade, letting the excess glaze run down the sides. Smooth the glaze over the top and sides of the roulade. Pick up any excess glaze on the waxed paper with the spatula for reglazing any bare spots. Using a wide spatula, transfer the roulade to a chilled oblong serving platter and freeze for 5 minutes to set the glaze.

Garnish:

9. Garnish the roulade with chocolate leaves and twigs. Dust with cocoa and confectioners' sugar. Serve the cake immediately.

Advance preparation: The roulade can be made up to one week in advance, wrapped tightly in plastic wrap, then aluminum foil, and frozen. Glaze and garnish the cake just before serving.

MAKES 12–15 SERVINGS

At right: Frango Mint Chocolate Alexander

MARSHALL FIELD'S FAMOUS FRANGO MINT CHOCOLATE ICE CREAM PIE

Nostalgia is personified in this Walnut Room tradition. How many Chicagoans remember this scrumptious frozen treat as their first restaurant dessert?

CRUST
1½ cups graham cracker
   crumbs (about 14 crackers)
6 tablespoons unsalted butter,
   melted
¼ cup sugar

FILLING
½ cup sugar
1½ teaspoons cornstarch
⅛ teaspoon salt
1 cup milk
8 Frango Mint Chocolates
   (milk) (about 3 ounces),
   chopped fine (about ½ cup)
1 large egg, at room
   temperature
1 cup heavy (whipping) cream
½ teaspoon vanilla extract

TOPPING
½ cup sugar
½ cup toasted, skinned, and
   coarsely chopped hazelnuts
   (about 2 ounces) (see index)

GARNISH
Whipped cream

At left: Marshall Field's Famous Frango Mint Chocolate Ice Cream Pie

Make the crust:

1. Position a rack in the center of the oven and preheat to 350°F. Butter a 9-inch pie pan. Combine graham cracker crumbs, melted butter, and sugar in a food processor fitted with a metal blade and process until well blended. Press mixture evenly and firmly into the bottom and sides of the pan. Bake until the crust is beginning to brown, about 8 minutes. Transfer the crust in the pan to a wire rack and cool completely.

Make the filling:

2. In a heavy-bottomed medium saucepan, combine the sugar, cornstarch, and salt. Add ¼ cup of the milk and whisk until the cornstarch is dissolved. Add the chopped chocolates and the remaining ¾ cup milk and cook over medium-low heat, stirring constantly with a wooden spoon, until the mixture comes to a boil, about 4 minutes. Remove the pan from the heat.

3. In a small bowl, whisk the egg until lightly beaten. Gradually add about ¼ cup of the hot chocolate mixture to the egg, whisking constantly until blended. Whisk the chocolate and egg mixture back into the saucepan and cook over very low heat, stirring constantly with a wooden spoon, until slightly thickened, about 1 minute. Do not let the mixture come near the boil, or the eggs will scramble. Transfer the custard to a medium bowl and let cool completely, stirring occasionally. Stir in the cream and vanilla. Refrigerate the custard until well chilled, about 2 hours.

4. Freeze the custard in an ice cream maker according to the manufacturer's instructions. Transfer the ice cream to the cooled crust and smooth the top with a cake spatula. Cover the pie tightly with plastic wrap and freeze until very firm, at least 4 hours or overnight.

Make the topping:

5. Butter a baking sheet. In a heavy-bottomed small saucepan, combine the sugar and hazelnuts and cook the mixture over medium heat, stirring constantly with a wooden spoon, until the sugar starts to dissolve, about 2 minutes. Reduce the heat to low and continue stirring until the hazelnuts are well coated and the sugar is caramelized. (Some of the sugar may remain unmelted.) Pour the caramelized hazelnuts out onto the prepared baking sheet. Transfer the baking sheet to a wire rack and cool completely.

6. Using your hands, break the cooled hazelnut praline into small pieces and transfer the praline to a food processor fitted with a metal blade. Pulse the mixture until finely chopped.

Assembly:

7. Sprinkle the top of the pie with the chopped hazelnut praline, pressing the praline in gently to adhere. Garnish with whipped cream. Serve immediately.

Advance preparation: The ice cream pie can be made up to one week in advance, with the praline topping, covered tightly with plastic wrap, then aluminum foil, and frozen.

MAKES 6–8 SERVINGS

FRANGO GRANDE CRYSTAL PALACE SUNDAE

The simplest things in life are often the best, and this minty chocolate sundae is simply grand.

2 large scoops Marshall
   Field's Vanilla Ice Cream
3 tablespoons Frango Mint
   Liqueur
Sweetened whipped cream for
   garnish (optional)
Frango Mint Liqueur for
   garnish (optional)
1 Frango Thin Mint

Place the ice cream in a large, chilled, stemmed goblet and pour on the 3 tablespoons liqueur. Top with a dollop of whipped cream and drizzle with additional liqueur if desired. Top with the Frango Thin Mint and serve immediately.

MAKES 1 SERVING

THE GROWN-UP'S FRANGO ICE CREAM SODA

One of the best reasons for being an adult is this sparkling soda
fountain favorite that has the added kick of
Frango Mint Liqueur.

3 tablespoons Frango Mint
   Liqueur
1 tablespoon chocolate syrup
2 tablespoons plus 1 large
   scoop Marshall Field's
   Chocolate Ice Cream
1 cup cold club soda
   (preferably seltzer from a
   syphon)

Pour the liqueur into a tall, chilled 10-ounce glass. Add the
chocolate syrup and 2 tablespoons of ice cream and, using a long spoon, stir
the ingredients until the ice cream is almost melted. Slowly pour in the cold
club soda. Place the scoop of ice cream on the lip of the glass, halfway into
the soda. Serve immediately with a straw and a long spoon.

MAKES 1 SERVING

TWO-TONE ICE CREAM BOMBE

A fudgy brownie base with a molded chocolate and vanilla ice cream dome that is sure to become a family favorite.

BROWNIE BASE

½ cup (1 stick) unsalted butter, cut up

2 ounces unsweetened chocolate, chopped fine

2 large eggs, at room temperature

1 cup sugar

1 teaspoon vanilla extract

½ cup flour

⅛ teaspoon salt

15 Frango Mint Chocolates (milk) (about 5½ ounces), chopped coarse (about 1¼ cups)

BOMBE

½ gallon store-bought chocolate ice cream, slightly softened

1 pint store-bought vanilla ice cream, slightly softened

15 Frango Mint Chocolates (milk) (about 5½ ounces), chopped coarse (about 1¼ cups)

Make the brownie base:

1. Position a rack in the center of the oven and preheat to 350°F. Butter an 8-inch round baking pan that is 1½ inches deep. Line the bottom of the pan with a circle of kitchen parchment or waxed paper.

2. In a heavy-bottomed, medium saucepan over low heat, melt the butter. Remove from heat, add the chopped unsweetened chocolate, and stir until the chocolate is melted. Let the mixture cool until tepid.

3. Using a hand-held electric mixer set at medium speed, beat the eggs in a medium bowl until light and thickened, about 2 minutes. Gradually add the sugar, then beat for an additional minute. Beat in the melted chocolate mixture and vanilla. Using a rubber spatula, fold in the flour and salt. Fold in the chopped chocolates. Spread the batter evenly in the prepared pan.

4. Bake until a toothpick inserted halfway between the center and the edge of the brownie base comes out with a moist crumb, about 35 to 40 minutes. Do not overbake; brownies should be moist. Transfer the brownie base in the pan to a wire rack and cool completely.

Make the bombe:

5. Line an 8-cup round metal bowl (preferably with an 8-inch diameter) with plastic wrap, letting the excess plastic hang over the sides.

6. Using a wooden spoon, spread the chocolate ice cream in an even layer along the sides and bottom of the prepared bowl, leaving a 1-inch border at the top of the bowl and making a well in the center. Freeze the bowl until the ice cream is firmer, about 15 minutes.

7. Combine the vanilla ice cream and chopped chocolates in a medium bowl until well combined. Fill the center well of the bombe with the vanilla ice cream mixture. Place the cooled brownie base on the ice cream inside the bowl and press down slightly to adhere. (Trim the brownie base with a sharp knife, if necessary, to fit the inside of the bowl.) Lift the ends of the plastic wrap up, cover the bombe, and freeze for at least 8 hours or overnight.

8. Just before serving, dip the outside of the bowl in cold water for about 5 seconds. Dry the bowl and peel back the plastic wrap. Invert the bowl onto a serving platter and unmold, removing the plastic wrap. Place the bombe in the refrigerator for 5 minutes to soften the ice cream very slightly. Using a sharp knife, cut the bombe into wedges.

Advance preparation: The bombe can be made, covered in plastic wrap, and frozen up to two days in advance.

MAKES 8–10 SERVINGS

FROZEN PROFITEROLES WITH BITTERSWEET SAUCE

Tiny cream puffs are filled with minted ice cream and served in
a pool of deep, dark bittersweet chocolate sauce.

PROFITEROLES

½ cup water

4 tablespoons unsalted butter,
cut into 4 pieces

⅛ teaspoon salt

½ cup flour

2 large eggs plus 1 large egg
yolk, at room temperature

GLAZE

1 large egg yolk

1 teaspoon water

BITTERSWEET SAUCE

6 ounces bittersweet chocolate,
chopped fine

⅔ cup water

1½ pints Frango Chocolate-
Flecked Ice Cream (see
index) or store-bought
vanilla ice cream

Fresh mint leaves for garnish

Make the profiteroles:

1. Position a rack in the center of the oven and preheat to 400°F.

2. In a medium saucepan, bring the water, butter, and salt to a full
boil over medium heat. Time the boiling of the water so the water comes

153

to a boil just as the butter melts. Remove the pan from the heat and stir in the flour. Return the saucepan to low heat and cook, stirring constantly with a wooden spoon, until the dough forms a ball and leaves a thin film on the bottom of the saucepan, about 1 minute. Remove the saucepan from the heat and let the dough cool slightly, stirring often, for about 2 minutes. One at a time, beat in the eggs and egg yolk until the mixture is smooth. Transfer the mixture to a pastry bag fitted with a large plain tip, such as Ateco Number 5. Pipe the mixture into 18 high mounds about 1½ inches in diameter.

Make the glaze:

3. Whisk together the egg yolk and water in a small bowl until mixed. Using a pastry brush, lightly brush each mound with some of the glaze, tapping down the points on top of the mounds and taking care not to let the glaze drip down the sides of the dough.

4. Bake until the profiteroles are golden brown, about 30 minutes. (To test for doneness, remove one profiterole from the oven. If it collapses within a minute, bake longer.) Using the tip of a sharp knife, pierce each profiterole, return the baking sheet to the oven, and continue baking for 5 minutes. Cool the profiteroles on the baking sheet for 5 minutes, then transfer to a wire rack to cool completely.

Make the sauce:

5. In a double boiler over hot—not simmering—water, melt the chopped bittersweet chocolate with the water, stirring occasionally, until smooth. Remove the double boiler from the water and let the sauce cool to room temperature.

Assembly:

6. Using a sharp knife, slice each profiterole in half horizontally. Fill each profiterole with about 2 tablespoons of the ice cream and replace the top of the profiteroles. Place the profiteroles in the freezer until ready to serve.

7. Divide the sauce among six dessert plates. Arrange three profiteroles in a triangle pattern on top of the sauce on each plate and place a sprig of mint in the center of each arrangement. Serve immediately.

Advance preparation: The profiteroles can be made and filled, wrapped airtight and frozen, up to two days in advance. The bittersweet chocolate sauce can be made up to two days in advance. Reheat the sauce carefully over hot water and cool to room temperature before serving.

MAKES 6 SERVINGS

FRANGO ALMOND CHOCOLATE BANANA POPS

A crunchy, nut-studded chocolate shell coats a frozen banana for
the perfect anytime snack.

4 ripe bananas, peeled
30 Frango Almond
Chocolates (about 11
ounces), chopped fine
(about 2 cups)

1½ cups toasted slivered
almonds (see index),
chopped coarse
8 wooden popsicle sticks
(available in toy stores)

1. Cut each banana in half vertically. Place each banana half on a
wooden popsicle stick and arrange each on a waxed paper–lined baking
sheet. Freeze until firm, at least 1 hour.

2. In the top of a double boiler over hot—not simmering—water,
melt the chocolates, stirring occasionally until smooth. Remove the top part
of the double boiler from the water.

3. Place the chopped almonds in a shallow baking dish. Dip each
frozen banana half in the melted chocolate, then roll in the chopped nuts.
Return the coated pops to the prepared baking sheet and refreeze until the
coating is firm, about 30 minutes.

Advance preparation: The banana pops can be made, covered in plastic
wrap, and frozen for up to five days.

MAKES 8 SERVINGS

HOT CHOCOLATE
A LA MENTHE

All you need is a cup of milk, a few Frango Chocolates, and a blender to make this quick pick-me-up. A dollop of whipped cream and a drizzle of green crème de menthe make it special.

1 cup milk
6 Frango Mint Chocolates
    (milk) (about 2 ounces)
Whipped cream for garnish
    (optional)
½ teaspoon green crème de
    menthe for garnish
    (optional)

In a small saucepan over medium heat, bring the milk just to the simmer. Place the chocolates in a blender, add the hot milk, and process for about 15 seconds, until the chocolates are melted and the mixture is smooth. Pour into a mug and, if desired, top with a dollop of whipped cream and drizzle the crème de menthe over the top of the cream. Serve immediately.

MAKES 1 SERVING

FRANGO CAFÉ AU LAIT

A steaming European beverage made in the Frango style, it can easily be "spiked" with your favorite spirit if desired.

1 cup milk
3 Frango Coffee Chocolates
   (about 1 ounce)
2 teaspoons instant espresso
   powder or regular instant
   coffee powder to taste
1 tablespoon brandy, rum,
   Kahlua, or Crème de
   Cacao (optional)

In a small saucepan, bring the milk to a simmer over medium heat. Place the chocolates in a blender, add the hot milk, espresso, and liquor, if desired, and blend for about 15 seconds, until the chocolates are melted and the mixture is smooth. Pour into a mug and serve immediately.

MAKES 1 SERVING

FRANGO MINT CHOCOLATE ALEXANDER

One sip of this frothy, ice-cold libation will soothe
the soul in seconds.

6 large ice cubes
4 tablespoons Frango Mint
  Liqueur
2 tablespoons brandy
¼ cup Marshall Field's
  Vanilla Ice Cream
Chocolate curls for garnish
(optional)

In a blender, process the ice cubes and liqueur until the ice cubes
are crushed. Add the brandy and ice cream and blend until smooth. Pour
into a chilled, stemmed glass and serve immediately. Garnish with chocolate
curls if desired.

MAKES 1 SERVING

RUM AND CHOCOLATE EGGNOG

This frothy, spirited beverage definitely should not be reserved for holidays. Simple to make, it's a perfect drink for crowds during any season.

30 Frango Rum Chocolates
   (11 ounces), chopped fine
   (about 2 cups)
6 large eggs, separated, at
   room temperature
1 cup sugar
1 cup amber rum, brandy, or
   whiskey
4 cups milk
2 cups heavy (whipping)
   cream

1. In a double boiler over hot—not simmering—water, melt the chopped chocolates, stirring occasionally, until smooth. Remove the double boiler from the water and let the chocolate cool until tepid.

2. In a medium bowl, using a hand-held electric mixer set at medium-high speed, beat the egg yolks with the sugar until thick and light in color, about 2 minutes. Beat in the rum. Beat in the melted chocolate until smooth. Beat in the milk and cream.

3. Using a hand-held electric mixer with clean, dry beaters and set at low speed, beat the egg whites in a grease-free large bowl until they start to foam. Gradually increase the speed to high and continue beating until the egg whites form stiff, shiny peaks. Fold the chocolate mixture into the egg whites. Tightly cover with plastic wrap and refrigerate until well chilled, at least 2 hours.

Advance preparation: The eggnog can be made up to one day in advance and refrigerated, covered tightly with plastic wrap.

MAKES 12 1-CUP SERVINGS

APPENDIX

CHOCOLATE DECORATIONS

PREPARATION

When making milk, dark, or white chocolate shavings and curls, keep two factors in mind:

1. Use a large chunk of chocolate, such as "break-up" chocolate or bulk chocolate, or a 1-ounce square from packaged supermarket chocolate.

2. The chocolate must be at the proper temperature, which is warm room temperature. If the chocolate is too cold, it will splinter and not curl. If your first attempts at curls and shavings splinter, warm the chocolate using either of these techniques:

- Place the chocolate directly under a hot light bulb for about 5 minutes, until the surface of the chocolate is warm but not melting; or
- Warm the chocolate in a microwave oven set at medium (50%) energy level for 30 seconds.

CHOCOLATE SHAVINGS

Using a large, sharp chef's knife, make very thin vertical cuts, "shaving" off thin pieces of chocolate as you proceed. Pick up the shavings with the knife and transfer to a waxed paper–lined baking sheet. Refrigerate the shavings until ready to use.

CHOCOLATE CURLS

Using a swivel-bladed vegetable peeler, make the chocolate curls by pressing down while you "peel" along the smooth side of the chocolate chunk. The harder you press, the thicker the curls. Let the curls fall onto a waxed paper–lined baking sheet, then refrigerate the curls until ready to use.

CHOCOLATE LEAVES

In the top part of a double boiler over hot—not simmering—water, melt 2 to 4 ounces of semisweet or bittersweet chocolate, stirring occasionally until smooth. Use firm, clean nontoxic leaves such as lemon, ivy, galax, or camellia. Using the back of a spoon, coat the underside of the leaves evenly and thinly with the melted chocolate. Refrigerate the leaves on a waxed paper–lined baking sheet for about 15 minutes, until the chocolate is firm. Carefully peel the leaves away from the chocolate. Refrigerate the leaves until ready to use.

TO TOAST ALMONDS, PECANS, AND WALNUTS

Place the nuts in a single layer on a baking sheet and bake in a preheated 350°F oven for 8 to 10 minutes, shaking the sheet a couple of times, until the nuts are lightly browned and fragrant. Let the nuts cool completely before chopping.

TO TOAST AND SKIN HAZELNUTS

Place the hazelnuts in a single layer on a baking sheet and bake in a preheated 350°F oven for 8 to 10 minutes, shaking the sheet a couple of times, until the skins are peeling and the hazelnuts are golden brown beneath the skins. Wrap the hazelnuts in a clean kitchen towel and let stand for 20 minutes. Using the towel, rub off the skins. (Stubborn skins can be removed by rubbing the hazelnuts against a fine-meshed sieve.)

INDEX